COLLECTED ESSAYS

COLLECTED ESSAYS

Kettering Foundation International Residents

Kettering Foundation Press

7. Strategies for Creating a Friendly Environment in an Unfriendly World
   by Alina Starinets   118

8. Cross-Cultural Management of International Education
   by Zhang Chunping   140

9. The Rural Issue in Colombia at the National and Local Levels
   by Angela Navarrete-Cruz   150

10. "Who Are We?"
    by Guo Jie   175

11. An Interview with Maureen Gillon
    by Maura Casey   193

Foreword

by
Maxine Thomas

Some of the rich contributions to research at the Kettering Foundation come from the many visitors and residents who stay at the foundation for short periods of time and work on ideas related to the research of the foundation, but considered through their own lenses of practice and place. This is true whether the visitor is from the United States or from another country.

The pieces in this book are excerpted or adapted from reports on research projects conducted by some of our international fellows during their stay at the foundation. They are intended, among other things, to provide ideas, guidance, and inspiration for those who come after them. The subjects are as varied and far-flung as the fellows themselves, although a surprising number of them deal with the problems of minority groups seeking civic agency. They reflect the learning that grew out of their stay and their research in their home countries.

Some of these fellows chose topics that illuminate problems of critical interest in their own parts of the world. Tendai Murisa from Zimbabwe and Angela Navarrete-Cruz from Colombia write about the need for agrarian reform and illuminate the struggles of small-holder rural populations in Africa and in Colombia to gain a significant say in the agricultural policymaking of their countries. Leonardo Neves Correa introduced Kettering to a completely new audience. He explores controversies over education for the deaf in his native Brazil. Each of these authors uses the experience to build upon skills derived from earlier experience with KF and honed in their immersive research while in residence.

Three of our Chinese fellows pursued interests in the American judicial system. Liu Hui examines the changing political factors that influenced the choice of US Supreme Court justices throughout the history of the court. Zhai Guoqiang analyzes the intricate differences underlying the structure and implementation of the US and Chinese Constitutions, while Jing Zhou takes on the question of whether the Equal Protection Doctrine as implemented in the United States could be applied to judicial practice in China.

Cross-cultural matters occupy the thoughts of Alina Starinets from Russia and Zhan Chunping from China. Starinets writes about racial and ethnic tensions in both Russia and the United States, with a focus on the problems of migrants who come to Russia from former Soviet republics. Zhan's two-part essay explores ways of improving the experiences of foreign students enrolled in international programs of Chinese and US universities and examines the experiences of immigrants in the United States in seeking to answer the question of whether America is "still a melting pot."

Guo Jie describes a related aspect of the immigrant experience in her essay entitled, "Who Are We?", a study of the multiple ways Latin Americans identify themselves in this country. Harley Eagle, a native North American, tells the story of a cross-cultural experience that illustrates the bonds between a Maori community in New Zealand and Native American peoples in North America.

Finally, an interview with New Zealander Maureen Gillon directly chronicles the connections between what she learned during her time at the Kettering Foundation and her work in the health-care and educational communities of her native Porirua, particularly in giving voice to heretofore disenfranchised segments of the population in and around the city.

Of necessity, the work that is presented here is a snapshot of an ongoing conversation among international residents and Kettering staff. Its utility and impact on the foundation's larger research is only partially clear now but some of these ideas have gone on to greatly influence our multinational work, as well as to put many of our research inquiries in a fuller context. It is with pleasure that I offer this volume for your review and hope there will be something that enhances your own work.

Maxine Thomas, Vice President
Kettering Foundation

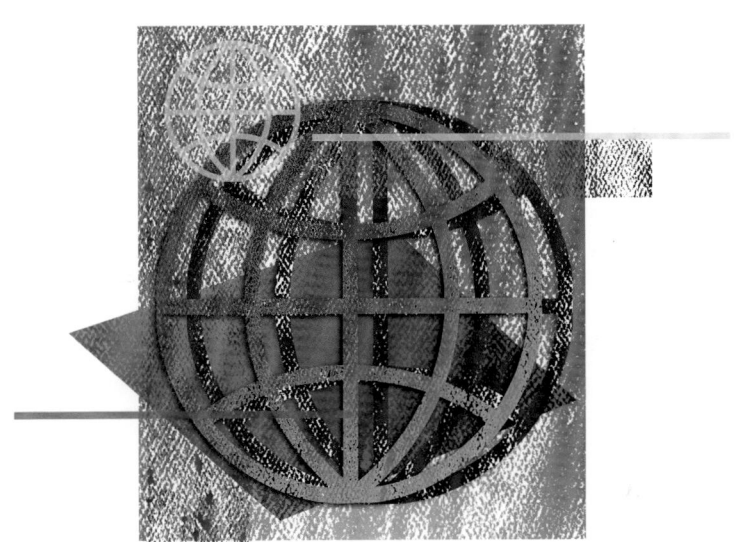

1

Implementation of the Chinese and US Constitutions: A Comparative Study

by
Zhai Guoqiang

Like the United States, China has a written constitution. Many scholars think that the Chinese Constitution exists in name only. But, because they use American constitutional theories to evaluate the Chinese Constitution, these scholars cannot effectively describe it.

In the past 30 years or more, China has been basically successful in transforming its society and is notable for having maintained social stability, for maintaining economic growth, and for improving people's lives. The Chinese Constitution, at present, differs in orientation from the centralism reflected in the Soviet model and also differs from the Western democratic model; it is difficult to explain the Chinese constitutional system using Western terminology. Therefore, academic circles need to treat this "socialist legal system with Chinese characteristics"[1] under the guidance of the party in power, seriously. In the past 30-plus years, the Chinese Constitution has not performed what would be called the normative function; rather it has mainly performed the function of providing principles of political guidance. This Constitution has reflected the mainstream ideology and changes in the nation's basic economic system. From 1949 to the present, the Constitution has mainly provided political guidance principles or manifestos, but that is not all there is to it. In fact, together with progress in developing rule of law in China, the Chinese Constitution has had the effect of bringing legal standards into play. More and more state organs and departments have gradually begun to view the Constitution as a legal norm.

There is no model in which a single main body implements the Constitution; all state organs have the duty to implement the Constitution. In the United States, the judicial branch plays an important role in the interpretation and implementation of the Constitution, but Congress and the administrative branches also implement the Constitution within the limits of their powers. Similarly, in China different organs have the power and duty to implement the Constitution. In fact, the document stipulates that all state organs, party organizations, and social groups have the duty to implement the Constitution. Generally speaking, Western scholars describe the Chinese system of government as a centralized system. In reality, authority is distributed among the different systems and ministries. As in the United States, different departments in China have different understandings and interpretations of constitutional issues. As a result, there is also the need for constitutional dialogue between different governmental branches.

In the United States, the majority of constitutional disputes are solved through judicial review. This is a systemic arrangement designed to solve political problems through legal procedures. This type of constitutional dialogue is developed around judicial review; the courts play a leading role. However, the courts are not the only leading organ; other organs also organize platforms for dialogue within the limits of their powers. Even if it is the court that explains the Constitution during actual cases, the political departments, various social organizations, interest groups, and the public also participate in constitutional dialogues. Furthermore, sometimes this kind of dialogue occurs outside the court. For example, for those political problems not believed to involve judgment, constitutional dialogue is mainly carried out through political departments. This paper will try to analyze the dialogue mechanism in the implementation of the Chinese Constitution through comparison with the constitutional system of the United States.

Comparing the Basic Structures of the Constitutions of China and the United States

China is a densely populated, developing country. Deng Xiaoping summarized the situation in China as "large population, thin foundation." The general theory is that the social structure of traditional China is hierarchical.[2] Confucian doctrine used to be the mainstream social view, but traditional social values and views have been attacked, changed, and even destroyed in the past 100 years. The Cultural Revolution brought about unprecedented destruction of China's traditional culture. On the whole, present-day China is still in the process of transforming from a traditional society to a modern society. There has never been a Western-style constitutional system established in China. Although there was a constitution when the Kuomingtang was in control of China, it was not effectively implemented throughout the country. After 1949, the Chinese Communist Party tried to overthrow the whole Kuomintang legal system so as to establish a socialist constitutional system. Consequently, it borrowed constitutional theory and practice from the Soviet Union and combined it with the governing experiences of the Chinese Communist Party during its revolution, to shape the constitutional system of today's China. There are two main differences between the structure of the Chinese and US Constitutions: the federalist system and the division of power, which separately embody a vertically and horizontally structured division of power.

Binary and Unitary Systems

The United States adopted a binary constitutional system. Each state has its own constitution, which establishes the governing system of the state government, including the legislative, judicial, and administrative organizations. The federal Constitution establishes the federal government system. Under the American federal system, the authority of the federal government comes from all the states. The states maintain a high degree of autonomy.

The Chinese Constitution supports a unitary system, which is different from the federal-state binary constitutional system in the United States.[3] According to the Chinese Constitution, the power of local organizations comes from the central government. If there are any differences, the local government must obey the decision of the central government. The Chinese Constitution emphasizes the unified order and does not admit local independent sovereignty. Under this system, local power comes from state-level law and is bestowed by the central government. The local governments have a certain amount of authority, but the division of power between the central government and the local government is not clear. The division of power between the American federal and state governments is clearer; the federal government and the states each implement the federal Constitution and each state implements its own constitution. (The US Supreme Court once asked a state superior court to interpret a connotation in its constitution.) Although China does not use the federal system as a principle for its Constitution, Chinese law allows the political and legal systems of Hong Kong and Macao Special Administrative Regions to be different from those on the mainland and these areas enjoy even greater sovereignty than the US states under the federal system. Thus, if one considers the relationship between the special administrative regions and the central government, it is somewhat questionable whether one can describe the Chinese government as a unitary constitutional system.

The structure of the Chinese Constitution is a compartmentalized (line-block) structure. Authority can go from the central government to the local base from top to bottom (line), but as far as specific organs and departments are concerned, they are subordinate to different localities (blocks). According to the Constitution, when different departments have different understandings of the Constitution, these are adjudicated by their common superior department. For example, when a difference occurs between the regulations set up by a State Council department and a local government, it can be reported to the State Council to be adjudicated. The important content of the US Constitution is to affirm the distribution of power between the states and the federal government, but there are no clear rules about the relationship between the central and the local governments in the Chinese Constitution. There is only a principled regulation: "The division of authority between the central and local state organizations follow the principle that under the unified leadership of the central government, local initiative and enthusiasm are to be fully developed." The local government enjoys a certain degree of sovereignty. Some reform measures that have violated the Constitution were called "benign violations of the Constitution."[4] At the present time, China is still in the process of reform. How to distribute authority between the central and local governments is an important problem facing the present and future of China.

Separation of Powers and Democratic Centralization

The United States, a governing system that calls for the separation of powers, is based on the theories of Locke and Montesquieu.[5] Under this system, the three different branches of the US government have a strict division of labor and maintain checks and balances on each other. The Chinese Constitution rejects the American model and instead practices the principle of democratic centralization with the People's Congress at its apex. According to the Chinese Constitution, democratic centralization is the basic principle for dealing with this vertical relationship. According to Deng Xiaoping, the main reason for not adopting the division of powers is that it is too involved and would lead to inefficiency. In a meeting with Korošec, a member of the Central Presidium of the Slovenian Communist Union, Deng Xiaoping pointed out:

> Our system is the People's Congress system. The People's democratic system under the Communist Party cannot have the Western type (separation of three powers). The superiority of a socialist country is that when doing something, when a resolution is made, it can be executed right away without any other involvement. When we say we want to reform the economic system, the whole country will execute it immediately; when we make a decision to establish special economic zones, we execute it right away without so much mutual involvement, no unresolved discussions, and no decisions without implementation.[6]

Although the Chinese Constitution rejects the separation of powers, it does not negate the reasonable division of authority. Although some scholars believe that the Chinese system combines legislative and executive functions, in reality the Chinese Constitution confirms different jurisdictions and the division of authority between different organizations. Therefore it might be viewed as a model of "separation of powers" with Chinese characteristics. However, this division of authority is mainly a vertical rather than horizontal one. Under this system, the judicial organs and the administrative organs are elected by the people's representative organ to whom they are responsible and by whom they are supervised. Administrative and judicial organs enjoy constitutional protection to independently exercise the functions and powers of their office. The Chinese constitutional system admits this kind of supervision from top to bottom, but it rejects the reverse supervision; it particularly rejects the judicial organs carrying out constitutional investigation of decisions made by legislative organs. However, judicial organs may carry out investigations into the legality of administrative actions, and representative organs can exercise supervision over judicial and administrative actions. Under the present distribution pattern of political authority though, there is still a lack of effective measures for representative organs to supervise the administration.

A "Confirmation Style" of Constitutional Amendment

Generally speaking, the US Constitution is believed to be the model of a rigid constitution; the procedure for amending it is very strict. There have been very few amendments since 1787 when the Constitution was drawn up.[7] The Chinese Constitution stipulates that the amendment procedure must be stricter than that used for changing ordinary laws, but, in fact, it is not too difficult to amend the Chinese Constitution. Since 1982, when the present Chinese Constitution was issued and implemented, it has been amended four times, mainly due to changes in mainstream political values and views. The party in power carried out confirmation of this kind of change through the Constitution. Some Chinese scholars call this way of amending the Constitution "policy-type constitutional amendment" or a "confirmation style of constitutional amendment."[8]

In the United States, the Constitution was drawn up first, and then the government was born in accordance with its precepts. In China, the government came first and then came the Constitution, which is one reason one cannot explain the Chinese Constitution using only the US constitutional concepts. Many Western scholars have noticed the differing characteristics of the Chinese and Western constitutions. The Chinese word *xiànfǎ* (for "constitution") cannot even be translated into *constitution*. The Chinese Constitution is not a social contract; it is a national declaration and thus more like the US Declaration of Independence. This kind of declaration is a confirmation of a triumphant political line. According to many scholars, the Western constitution possesses a strong legal binding force; the Chinese Constitution does not have so much legal meaning.[9] If the Constitution is viewed as a political declaration, then a so-called "violation of the Constitution" is naturally not a real problem. Therefore, some scholars have noted that, from a historical perspective, no matter whether it was the previous or the present Chinese government, whenever the Constitution became an obstacle to social development, the Constitution was amended, so it would not become an obstacle.[10] In the past 30 years, the changes to the Chinese Constitution have been mainly passive changes to adjust to political realities, embodying the model of a confirmation style of constitution. So the Constitution has not been viewed as a legal restriction for the government. Actually it has even been seen as a resource for the government.[11] Of course, this view of constitutional instrumentalism has been widely criticized by scholars.

During the Yan'an period, the Chinese Communist Party accepted the view that the main function of the Constitution was to confirm political reality. The classic expression is the definition by Mao Zedong in his article "Constitutionalism in the New Democracy":

> Constitutionalism around the world, no matter whether in Britain, France, the United States, or the Soviet Union, has been that after the success of revolution when there was the reality of democracy, then a fundamental great law was issued to recognize it. This then is the Constitution.[12]

If we trace back even further, the earliest source of this model of confirmation type of constitution came from the Constitution of the Soviet Union. In 1936, Stalin pointed out that the Constitution is a confirmation of facts; it is not a guiding principle. As he said about the draft Soviet Constitution:

> There is an important difference between guiding principles and the Constitution. What guiding principles talk about are things that do not exist yet; they are to be gained and won over. On the contrary, what the Constitution should talk about are things that are already in existence, and they are things already gained and won over. Guiding principles mainly talk about the future, but the Constitution talks about the present.[13]

Simply put, in this view, a constitution is a confirmation of facts, but to simply equate the function of the Constitution as a confirmation of the status quo seemed obviously too extreme to the Chinese. Thus, Chinese Communist Party theorists took the idea a step further. As Zhang Youyu pointed out, we must be careful that the so-called "things we have already gained and won over" refer to the basic mutual relationship of various social forces and the general facts of life for the whole society, but does not include all the individual and partially realized facts. Next, the so-called "already gained" is not limited to "completely realized," and includes not only the "must be" but the "may be" realized, particularly the parts that were restrained, restricted, and obstructed by the Constitution and "were not realized." For example, the 135th article of the new Soviet Union Constitution stipulates: "The election of representatives will adopt universal suffrage; those Soviet Union citizens of 18 years of age, no matter of what race, nationality, sex, religion, education level, period of residency, social background, condition of wealth and past activities, all have the right to participate in elections." That gives the right to vote to those missionaries and White Party members whose right to vote was stripped away. These were "must be" and "may be" realized facts, but their realization was obstructed by the old Constitution, which needed to be amended. If all the things that "must be" and "may be" realized need not be stipulated in the Constitution, then why not just keep the old Constitution. Why write a new one at all?[14]

In Chinese political thinking, this view of a confirmation constitution occupies the mainstream. The party in power views the Constitution as a kind of political symbol and sign; it is to be adjusted following changes in political reality. Although this view of the Constitution is the mainstream political view, both the party in power and nongovernmental scholars believe the implementation of the Constitution is an important part of the legal system in China. In the past 30-plus years, the Chinese Constitution has, to a certain degree, embodied the functions of a legal standard.

Implementation of the Chinese Constitution

In the context of the Chinese language, "implementation of the Constitution" is a very important concept, frequently mentioned in mainstream political discourse. To China, the Constitution is a modern product. Both during the Republican period and in post-1949 China, implementation was very much emphasized at the time the Constitutions were being formulated. The implementation of the 1982 Constitution is mainly political. Chinese constitutions have traditionally not been implemented as legal standards. In any case, the Constitution cannot implement itself; it has to rely on specific mechanisms to be implemented. According to the Chinese Constitution, the scope of implementing bodies is quite wide. It includes all the state organs, social organizations, and others.[15] As basic law, the implementation of the Chinese Constitution is achieved mainly through legislation.

Implementing the Constitution through Legislation

It is important that the Chinese Constitution carries out its realization through legislation. For example, some scholars believe that the socialist Constitution does not protect individual rights in the face of state power.[16] The written document does not have a clear stipulation about the structure of horizontal rights. However, the Chinese Constitution has established an administrative procedural system to protect this right. This system is thought of as the concrete implementation of Article 41 of the Chinese Constitution, which states that citizens have the right to appeal, to sue, or to report any state organization or staff who commit an action in violation of the law or who neglect their duties.

Unlike the US Constitution, the implementation of the Chinese Constitution mainly relies on legislative organs to carry out its precepts. When a legislative organ draws up laws, it usually stipulates in the general rules that "the drawing up of this law is based on the Constitution." This type of statement is rarely seen in legislation in other countries. A study of Chinese legislation since the implementation of the Constitution shows that the majority of legislation is the result of carrying out stipulations of the Constitution. The concrete ways in which this is done include:

> (1) framing legislation, to set various organizational standards and procedural standards for the operation of state power. Compared to the US Constitution, the Chinese Constitution has more of a principle organizational procedural structure. This characteristic determines that the organizational and procedural standards of the Constitution require legislation to make them concrete. This legislation is not the same as the usual legislation carried out by legislative jurisdiction based on the Constitution. It can be thought of as a quasi-constitutional legal standard;

> (2) actually legalizing abstract basic rights into different types of legal rights and setting up different legal mechanisms in systems of public and private law—which sets up separate legal systems. On the one hand, it sets up a public system through legislation to safeguard rights and limit powers, such as administrative permit legislation, administrative enforcement legislation, and administrative punishment legislation. On the other hand, it sets up legislation to confirm the private legal system and define the limits of rights between equal principal parties;

> (3) setting up legislation to perfect the proactive system of safeguarding basic rights. Specifically, it sets up concrete legislation to confirm the required legal system for safeguarding basic rights, such as the judicial and appeal system, the social safeguard system, and the education system;

(4) setting up the legal limit of safeguarding basic rights. Basic rights stipulated in the Constitution are only declarations of principle, so legislation is required to set up legal definitions for the actual scope of various basic rights. However, due to the lack of a legal constitutional investigation procedure, there is still no constitutional standard for determining whether these legal limits are proper.

Implementation of the Constitution by Administrative Organs

In China, administrative power is the core of state power. Administrative organs set most of the organizational standards based on the Constitution, and they perform the function of standardizing power. In addition, as the "highest administrative organization" stipulated in the Constitution, the State Council makes decisions and, in some cases, redresses violations of the Constitution—for example, making judgments of unconstitutional behavior against local jurisdictions selling and renting collective-owned and state-owned land, or those that unilaterally set up nationality townships. Administrative organs can even make judgments regarding certain activities by judicial organs. For example, the People's Supreme Court at one point asked the Ministry of Land and Resources how to understand issues concerning city land.[17]

Implementation of the Constitution by Judicial Organs

Modern legal systems can be roughly divided into the common law system and the continental law system. The United States inherited the British common law tradition. In general, the Chinese legal system borrowed the European continental tradition of a written law. The Chinese court system is somewhat different from the European system. In the allocation of personnel and actual political position, the court and the People's Procuratorate are only equal to government departments. They are in a weaker position than the administrative organs.[18] Under this system, the judicial organs are elected by the People's Congress and are responsible to it. The main duty of judicial organs is to administer the laws of the highest legislative organs and not to overrule them. Under this system, the court, the People's Procuratorate, and the public security administrative departments are all looked upon as "dictator organs." Members of the court and the People's Procuratorate, for example, used to wear uniforms similar to those of the police. Since the year 2000, the judges' attire was changed from uniforms to robes similar to those of Western judges. However, Chinese judicial organs are weaker than legislative organs under the law and are also weaker than administrative organs in actual power. To a certain degree this influences the independence of trials by judicial organs. The recent new round of judicial reform tries to eliminate this influence through changes in the judicial system.

In China, the court has no authority to deal with constitutional issues and generally does not use the Constitution as the basis for trials. In 1955, the Supreme People's Court pointed out in one of its rulings that it was not appropriate to quote the Constitution in criminal cases. In 2001, however, the Supreme People's Court quoted the stipulation of the right of education in the Constitution in the judicial interpretation of a civil case. The Supreme People's Court abolished this judicial interpretation in 2008. Up to now, the Supreme Court has avoided any constitutional issues.

The Supreme Court of the United States explicitly judges the constitutionality of legislative and administrative actions, but the Chinese Court cannot make the same kinds of judgments. However, the Chinese court can exclude regulations that violate the Constitution by resorting to the selective use of legal rules, thus realizing constitutional control of the "judicial law system." Under the present judicial system, even though the court may use legal standards selectively, still "this will not affirm the efficacy of related legal documents."[19] Therefore the effective scope of this type of constitutional control is only in the judicial trial area. Furthermore, there is a lack of trial precedent to support it so the actual results are limited. The court can carry out legal interpretation of laws according to the Constitution in ordinary legal cases and thereby use the Constitution indirectly. If it discovers a law that violates the Constitution, the court can report it to concerned organizations of the Standing Committee of the National People's Congress to deal with it. The use of this method is similar to the system of the German common court asking the Constitutional Court to interpret the Constitution.

Informal Constitutional Review

According to the Chinese Constitution, the Standing Committee of the National People's Congress is mainly responsible for constitutional control. This function is similar to the function of the US Supreme Court or the German Federal Constitutional Court. This is a formal legal mechanism written into the law for constitutional control. However, up to now, legal organs have never legally abolished or revoked a decision, so the whole mechanism of constitutional control by law is in a dormant state. In actual legal practice, however, there exists an internal system at various levels of the Standing Committee of the National People's Congress that is regularly used as a mechanism for constitutional control. This method of solving legal standard violations of the Constitution is mainly designed "to strengthen communication and negotiation with the formulating organization, propose suggestions, and urge it to amend or abolish it." In the practice of the legal work of the Standing Committee of the National People's Congress, a legal question-and-answer system has gradually evolved. The 55th article of the "Legislative Law" affirms the legality of this type of systemic practice. According to the stipulations of this article, the working organs of the Standing Committee of the People's Congress may study and rule on actual legal issues. Many disputes have been resolved by this process of internal communication and negotiation. Some of the legal issues involve interpreting the text of the Constitution and the constitutionality of the conduct of governmental authority. Some legal organs in the People's Congress also interpret articles in the Constitution in some cases. This internal communication and coordination mechanism, which employs question-and-answer dialogue to determine constitutional issues in disputes arising from the exercise of governmental authority can be said to be a kind of internal and informal constitutional investigation.

Constitutional Differences and Dialogue between Different Departments

As noted, the Chinese Constitution is different from the Constitution of the United States. The Chinese Constitution carries out legal confirmation based on a fundamentally preformed system. This is a basic fact in the history of the development of the Chinese Constitution. When the Constitution of 1954 was drafted, the Common Program constituted its primary framework. According to Zhou Enlai, the major content of the Constitution should include three elements: the system of the country; its social structure; and people's rights. This material was already included in the Common Program. Related regulations that had already been implemented, or needed to be implemented, could be put in the Constitution. After some deliberation or amending of the Central Government Organization Law, it could also be put in the Constitution. The principles outlined in the Election Law could also be put in the Constitution. In this way, a complete Constitution could be organized.[20]

As a matter of fact, long before the Constitution was drafted, even before the Common Program was drafted, the Chinese Communist Party as a quasi-government was already exercising the function of managing society. During the process of drafting the Constitution, many different systems and departments were broadly mobilized to participate. Many of the members of the drafting committee were leaders of governmental departments. Some committee members of the Central Government Committee, members of the Chinese Political Consultative Council, and other departments also participated in the drafting of the Constitution.[21] After the Constitution was drafted, various departments carried out implementation of the Constitution within the scope of their assigned responsibilities. For example, the Departments of National Land and Resources were more professional in their interpretation and implementation of the articles concerning land systems, so judicial organs may direct inquiries to administrative organs for opinions with reference to such issues. Also, for example, the Land Department has the authority to interpret matters concerning city land-ownership systems stipulated in the Constitution, the Forestry Department's understanding of forestry rights in the Constitution is the most important opinion in deciding the meaning of related articles, and the Department of Post and Telecommunications has the authority to interpret matters regarding secrecy and freedom of communication.

Departmentalism in the Implementation of the Chinese Constitution

Although the American federal judiciary plays an important role in the process of implementing the Constitution, it is not the only body that interprets the Constitution. The legislative and administrative branches also implement the Constitution and interpret the meaning of the Constitution. According to Andrew Jackson, all three branches have the power to implement the Constitution within each one's designated scope of authority.[22] This departmentalism is the implementation of the US Constitution.

The division of the Chinese government into different departments or "systems" is the purview of the political party in power, rather than a system called for in the Constitution. The party carries out the administration of society through different governing departments, each having a close connection with its own administrative area, thus forming their own "systems." Under a planned economy, there were even direct subordinate relationships between the administrative management departments and the targets of management. This phenomenon is called "nonseparation of administration and industry" or "nonseparation of administration and society." Under this system, a managing department and its related area formed a system of its own. There is a certain level of independence and encapsulation between the elements of the system. Owing to the differences in division of labor and the fact that there is no subordinate relationship, it is very easy to have a situation in which each is in charge of itself. The American scholar Kenneth G. Lieberthal who studies Chinese politics, describes this system as "fragmented authoritarianism."[23] Under this system, there is division of labor between departments, but different departments all belong to a comprehensive organization—for example, a party committee or a senior-level government unit. The actual administrative authority mainly belongs to different departments, and the authority of the comprehensive organization is rather weak on the whole. In reality, there is a competitive relationship between the different systems in China, which has some of the function of division of labor and checks and balances. For example, we have the mutual supervision and checks and balances between the tobacco industry system and the public health system in the control of tobacco, and the competition and checks and balances between environmental protection departments and the economic management systems, even though these checks and balances are somewhat limited.

Historically, these different departments and organizations came into being before the Constitution. From the establishment of the People's Republic of China on October 1, 1949, to the opening of the First People's Congress in September 1954, China's government system adopted a mixed judicial and administrative structure. The Central Government organizations included the Central People's Governing Committee and the Government Administrative Council appointed and led by it, the People's Revolutionary Military Committee, the People's Supreme Court, the People's Procuratorate and other organizations. The organizational structures, confirmed by the Chinese Constitution, were mainly institutions already in existence. The drafting of the US Constitution occurred in just the opposite way. It came before the creation of legislative, judicial, and administrative departments. The administrative departments did not participate in the design and drafting of the Constitution. The mechanism for interpreting the Constitution did not constitute the authority of the departments. Owing to the fact that Chinese governmental departments existed before the Constitution, these departments all participated in the drafting and amending of the Constitution. Because of different specialties and divisions of labor, specific departments have greater rights to comment on certain articles of the Constitution. When a judicial organ is trying related cases, it will honor the interpretation by these organizations and will even inquire about the way these departments understand the Constitution.

The departments are the core of different systems, and there will be conflict of interest between systems and differences between departments. Under the decentralized and multivariate structure of implementation of the Constitution, different departments have different understandings of the Constitution. Each department has the authority to interpret those constitutional articles that relate to them, and other departments will honor their interpretations. For example, the State Council is a system composed of many departments. Although it is judicially and legislatively independent, its interior is decentralized and there are constant conflicts between departments. Simply put, the Chinese Constitution specifies a division of power but no formal system of checks and balances; the Chinese government, however has an informal system of checks and balances but no formal division of power.

A Coordinated Dialogue Mechanism

The Chinese Communist Party does not have the same general significance as Western parties do, and it fulfills different functions from American parties. In reality, it plays the function of a quasi-government. Historically, there was first the Communist Party and then the governmental organizations and then the Constitution. In the Western constitutional system, the party-organized system is not the core of the political organization and is not where authority lies. Under the American constitutional system, the three branches of government obtain their political authority from the Constitution. But in China, although legally the greatest authority is in the People's Congress, actual political authority lies in the Chinese Communist Party[24] and the organization of the party is the link between various organizations and specific systems. There are party organizations within all formal national organizations, and the basic-level party organizations are even spread to all aspects of society, including social organizations and industrial companies. Every government organization is responsible to the corresponding party organization.[25] Therefore, whether it is a legislative organization, a judicial organization, or an administrative organization, it will carry on consultation or dialogue through the working mechanism of the party.

Since the reform and opening up to the outside world, one of the important experiences of legal construction in China has been the party's retreat from the formal legal mechanism, and the transfer of actual power to the legislative organs, administrative organs, and the courts.[26] Under the model of fully unified responsibility of party and government administration, no matter whether a strategic decision is correct, responsibility is borne by the party. Since the reform, strategic decisions of the Chinese Communist Party have gradually been transferred from emphasis on substance to emphasis on process.[27] Hideo Tsuchiya calls it "decentralized leadership." Under the present system, the party leadership basically "assumes all responsibility for the overall situation and coordinates all departments." In the Chinese political system, effective coordination is an important embodiment of the ability to solve problems, and the people who work in the coordinating organizations have more opportunities for easier advancement. To an official, the ability to coordinate is even more important than specialized professional knowledge. Therefore, there has appeared the phenomenon of so-called "nonprofessionals leading professionals."

In the organization of the Chinese Communist Party, there are various types of coordinating organizations for discussion of official business. These coordinating organizations include both permanent and nonpermanent working (leading) groups. The coordination mechanism in the party is guided by various internal mechanisms, such as the Central Culture Committee or the Central Comprehensive Management Committee. Legislative organs, administrative organs, and judicial organs participating in this type of coordinating mechanism are called member units. These organizations may be divided into permanent and nonpermanent entities. Permanent leading groups, for example, are the Central Politics and Legal Affairs Committee, the Central Social Management and Innovation Committee, the Central Taiwan Affairs Leading Group, the Central Financial and Economic Affairs Leading Group, and the Central Foreign Affairs Leading

Group. The temporary leading groups are generally established to promote specific public policies of great importance. For example, the Central Judicial Reform Leading Group was established to promote judicial reform. Based on need, this type of temporary coordinating organization may be changed into a permanent one.

Coordinating Mechanisms Guided by the State Council

According to the Chinese Constitution, the legal position of the People's Congress is theoretically higher than that of administrative and judicial organs, and it enjoys legislative and supervisory authority as well as the power to interpret the Constitution. Since its authority became empty, however, it was once called the "rubber stamp." Although legislative power has increased in the past 30 years, the administrative organs have always been more important in political and legal practice in China. In the language of Chinese politics, "Party Central" and "State Council" are often mentioned together. In the majority of situations, the position of the responsible person in the administrative organ is often higher than that of a member or even a director of the People's Congress. As the highest administrative organization, the State Council will organize joint meetings as a dialogue and consultation mechanism. Different departments of administrative organs may have different understandings of the Constitution and these differences may be solved through various coordination mechanisms in the administrative system. In the United States, different administrative departments also may have different understandings and interpretations of constitutional issues. For example, in two cases related to the Federal Communication Commission (FCC), the opinion of the Attorney General and that of the commission were different, and in the end the court supported the opinion of the FCC.[28]

Similar to the organization of the Communist Party, the State Council has various kinds of permanent and nonpermanent coordination organs whose operating mechanisms are similar to that of the main party organization. Permanent organs are, for example, the State Council Legal System Office, the Poverty Alleviation and Development Leading Group Office and other such offices; nonpermanent organs would include, for example, the Leading Group for Breaking Up Sequential Indebtedness and its office. Here too, temporary leading group offices can be changed into permanent coordinating organizations as occurred, for example, with the State Council

Poverty Alleviation and Development Leading Group Office, the State Council Diversion of Water from South to North Office, and the Three Gorges Office, among others. These organizations perform the function of communication and coordination between various departments and systems. In addition, there is a relatively loose coordinating organization called Joint Meeting. According to stipulations of the State Council, the Joint Meeting is a kind of consultative organization. It is "a working mechanism established to consult and manage matters involving the duties of many departments. Membership is based on a commonly negotiated working system to communicate in a timely manner and to coordinate different opinions in order to promote the implementation of work assignments." At the same time, the State Council stipulates that "the establishment of interministerial joint meetings should be strictly controlled. Generally joint meetings will not be established for matters that can be coordinated and solved between the main department and other departments."

An official seal will not be created for the interministerial joint meetings and no formal documents will be transmitted. If there is a definite need for formal documentation, it may use the name of the leading department and use the official seal of that department, or the related member units can jointly issue formal documents. Depending on actual need, the member units of the Joint Meeting may include organizational units of the Communist Party or judicial organs. Because Chinese judicial organs have weaker political authority compared to comparable administrative organs, the dialogue and consultation between the judicial and administrative organs is mainly that of dialogue between the judicial organ and the administrative unit.

For example, according to the "Reply of the State Council Regarding Agreement to Establish an Interministerial Joint Meeting System for Serious and Extraordinary Work Safety Incident Investigation, Communication, and Coordination," the Interministerial Joint Meeting consists of the People's Procuratorate, the Ministry of Public Safety, the Justice Department, Safety Regulatory Headquarters, the Supreme Court, and the Supreme People's Procuratorate, with the Ministry of Supervision as the leading unit. Another example is: "The State Reply Letter of the State Council Regarding Agreement to Adjust the Duties and Member Units of the Interministerial Joint Committee for Constructing a Social Credit System (2012) No. 88": the leading units are the Development and Reform

Committee and the People's Bank; the convenors are the director of the Development and Reform Committee and the president of the People's Bank; the member units are the Central Party Secretariat, the Central Propaganda Ministry, the Central Political and Legal Affairs Committee, the Central Civilization Office, the Ministry of Supreme Supervision, the Ministries of Education, Supervision, Civil Affairs, Justice, Finance, Agriculture, Culture, and Health, the Bureau for Preventing Corruption, the Bureau of Public Employees, the Intellectual Property Rights Bureau, and the Food and Drug Inspection Bureau.

Other Unofficial Dialogue Mechanisms

There are many other coordinating organs as well. Some, such as the general offices of various levels of the party and the government, are comprehensive coordinating organs; others, such as some State Council offices, are specialized. When the opinions of departments differ, the coordinating organ can unify them by organizing consultations and discussions. This form of dialogue is mainly for unofficial coordinating conferences.

Moreover, any two organizations with no subordinate relationship may consult and carry on dialogues directly through the exchange of documents. This type of document is generally called a "letter." According to "The Work Regulations for Handling Official Documents of the Party and Government Administrative Organs" jointly announced by the Central General Office and the State Council General Office, this form of transmitting documents is mainly suitable for organizations who are not subordinate to each other to arrange work, exchange questions and answers, and seek approval or examination of matters. For example, a judicial organ and an administrative organ can carry on informal constitutional dialogue through direct letters and telegrams, as in the "Reply Letter of the State Land Administration Bureau Regarding Ownership and Use of City Residential Sites and Other Issues." Coordination in the form of official letters may be called "back and forth correspondence."

China is, in fact, a society based on human feelings and relationships; various types of informal meetings also constitute an important method of communication. Sometimes, officials even go so far as to use personal relationships to negotiate issues. In cases where "public affairs are managed in a private manner," the difficulty of coordination increases or decreases according to the nature of private relationships. (Thus it is not hard to understand why drinking becomes an important element in the process of Chinese political operations. The importance of alcohol is to "grease relationships.") Why do people make use of personal relationships to coordinate consensus? There are many reasons, but the main motivation is that one's career achievements determine the achievements of the organization, as well as one's own individual transfers and promotions. Moreover, government officials increase their own social capital in situations where there is no division between public and private. Sometimes, this unofficial system can enhance communication and dialogue to form consensus, thus becoming a beneficial supplement to the formal system. Sometimes, however, this informal system can be impractical or it may be a poor substitute for the formal negotiation system. There may be compromises that involve the sacrifice of principles. Therefore, it is necessary to try to restrict this means of informal coordination and to perfect the formal dialogue mechanism and platform.

The Judiciary as the Core of the Dialogue Mechanism

One important implementation mechanism of the US Constitution is judicial investigation of violations of the Constitution. This model has been adopted by many countries, including Japan, Canada, and Australia. Under this system, the judiciary has the power to investigate the legislative organ to determine constitutionality and to make authoritative interpretations of the Constitution in actual legal cases. In reality, judicial interpreting of the Constitution is not a system clearly regulated by the US Constitution; it is a systemic practice that started with the case of *Marbury v. Madison* in 1803. In the process of implementing the US Constitution, the judicial organ took up the function of safeguarding it as well. When different departments have different understandings of the Constitution, the judiciary, particularly the Supreme Court, interprets the meaning. In actual cases, the judiciary has the highest power to interpret the Constitution; the interpretation of the Constitution by the Supreme Court is final. But the interpretation by the court is not willful or arbitrary. Constitutional dialogue outside the court also has an important effect. During the judicial process, different organizations start up dialogues; participants are the Congress, the president, administrative organizations, the states, various interest groups, and even the general public.[30] During this judicial process, sometimes the participants speak as persons involved and sometimes as "friends of the court." The core constitutional dialogue at the Supreme Court occurs among the judges who make decisions on constitutional issues in closed-door discussions. The court makes a decision based on the opinions of the majority of its judges. However, judges with different opinions may also express minority opinions. These minority opinions may be accepted by the majority in the future and may become the theoretical basis of a new decision. This constitutional dialogue around the judicial process avoids arbitrary rulings based on a single judge's personal values. Many scholars do not agree with Chief Justice Hughes' view that the meaning of the Constitution should be decided by the court. These critics hold that the judges' interpretation should be restricted by other departments and even the public's understanding of the Constitution.[31]

In the United States, judicial investigation of constitutional violations supplies an effective process for consultation and communication. This dialogue is guided by the judiciary but the participants are not limited to the judiciary. In the Chinese constitutional system, the judicial organ is the People's Congress, which is also the executive organ. The Chinese Constitution is a political constitution. It produces its effect mainly by political techniques. In the view of mainstream political thinkers the judicial organ is not suited to solve constitutional issues because constitutional issues are political and these issues should be given over to a higher political authority to solve. As noted above, the judicial organ does not have higher political authority. An important characteristic for the implementation of the Constitution is to deal with the constitutional issues as legal issues by using nonlegal methods. If we say that in the United States all political issues will become legal issues sooner or later, it is just the opposite in China where any legal issue may become a political issue, which may be resolved through informal systems. This kind of constitutional dialogue can be called a coordination mechanism.

This Chinese-style coordination mechanism is just the opposite of the US principles of division of power and checks and balances. Thus, US judicial constitutional theory cannot be used to accurately describe the actual operation of the Chinese constitutional system. There are certain limitations even for using the functional framework of the legislative, the judicial, and the administrative division of power to describe the Chinese Constitution. Only when these are combined with other functions and organizations can one fully and accurately describe the operation of the Chinese Constitution. The key to understanding the Chinese Constitution is not as a judicial organ, but as the practice of the Constitution beyond the court. Comparatively speaking, implementation of the Chinese Constitution is not carried out through the judicial process.

A Constitutional Dialogue Mechanism Goes Beyond the Judicial

Although the American judiciary plays an important role in the process of implementing the Constitution, it is not the only organ for interpreting and implementing the Constitution: all federal and state governmental organs have these duties. As far as the implementation of the US Constitution is concerned, the federal Supreme Court, Congress, and administrative departments are all primary participants in the implementation of the Constitution. The various legislative, judicial, and administrative organs are also primary participants in the implementation of the Constitution. Scholars have called this coordinate construction of the Constitution.[32] Different departments may have different understandings and interpretations of the Constitution; they carry out coordination or dialogue among themselves. Not only different departments at the federal level, but all the states have different implementations of the federal Constitution. In the United States, it is up to the judiciary to sort out conflicts when they arise. In China, there are also different interpretations of the Constitution between different departments, but the main channel of constitutional dialogue is not judicial investigation; it is through the coordination mechanism outside of the legal mechanism.

In the United States as well, the judiciary is not the only channel for constitutional dialogue. If political departments have different opinions about constitutional judgments by the judiciary, they may respond within the scope of their respective official powers. Social organizations and the general public may also engage in public discussions although this constitutional dialogue is one that takes place outside the judicial arena. Liberal constitutional scholars view the court as a "principle forum," but in reality when it meets certain conditions, the legislative organ can also be a principle forum. Congress can initiate dialogue around constitutional implementation, especially on so-called "political issues" which the court recognizes as not being judicial in nature. During this dialogue process, various committees function as vehicles to initiate the constitutional dialogue and carry out constitutional investigation on the legal draft.

This investigation is rather similar to the pre-investigation by legal committees of Chinese legislative organs. This dialogue mechanism mainly deals with constitutional issues through judicial committees of the legislative assembly, but this kind of dialogue also exists widely in other committees. The main body mostly concentrates on safeguarding basic rights.[33] Similarly, the legislative hearing process of the US Congress relies heavily on the participation of administrative organs, social groups, constitutional scholars, and interest groups.[34]

US administrative organs enjoy wide official power in the implementation of the Constitution. They carry out constitutional dialogue through participation in the legislative program and the judicial process. The former, for example, is through expressing opinions on the constitutionality of bills in the Congress and even during the signing of the legislation.[35] The latter, for example, is through participating in lawsuits as a concerned party. When there are different understandings of constitutional issues between Congress and the administration, the judiciary often takes a passive position and refuses to get involved.

Under the division of powers in the United States, the constitutional dialogue is a horizontal dialogue between three equal bodies.[36] Because there is no subordinate relationship, the three government branches rarely have direct dialogue and consultation concerning constitutional issues. This strict division of power also may cause related departments to have difficulty coordinating well and to experience a reduction in efficiency. Public-opinion polling has revealed that many people expect the three branches to have direct consultation and dialogue. As it stands, constitutional dialogue among the three branches is mostly from a kind of historical development perspective.

The Chinese constitutional dialogue, however, is oriented towards specific issues. The relationship of the Chinese legislative, administrative, and judicial organs is not a horizontal relationship. As a "super legislative organ," the position of the People's Congress is higher than that of both judicial and administrative organs. As far as constitutional issues are concerned, the interpretation of the Constitution by the Standing Committee of National People's Congress (SCNPC) has a greater effect than interpretations by the judicial and administrative organs. According to the Constitution and the legislative law, the administrative organ and the judicial organ should hand over constitutional issues to the SCNPC. During this process, consultation on constitutional issues is carried out between the different organizations, producing a vertical constitutional dialogue.

The American dialogue emphasizes checks and balances so it is easy to have a stalemate. When participants become deadlocked, they can only transfer the dispute to another procedure to continue the consultation. For example, when the legislative organ does not agree with the interpretation of the Constitution by the court, they can launch a new process.

The fundamental principle in the establishment of the Chinese Constitution is a "democratic centralization system." Different organizations all belong to the same political core so there is no requirement for checks and balances between them. This constitutional dialogue is nonantagonistic. Chinese traditional culture values harmony, not disrupting good feelings, and stresses unity. If obvious differences occur between different organizations, they will not be approved by the mainstream political culture. Even for some unconstitutional actions, the organization with power will solve them through nonantagonistic internal consultation mechanisms. Peng Zhen once pointed out: "It is not easy to ask everyone to do things according to law now, since we have not stressed the legal system for a few thousand years. Therefore, for some issues, the Standing Committee of the National People's Congress just finds ways to remind them. As long as they are corrected, it will be just fine."[37] Therefore, the way of handling cases of constitutional violation is not to directly proclaim a violation; it is to carry out internal dialogue and consultation. And then the organization that made unconstitutional decisions will take the initiative to withdraw them. For example, the method of dealing with the Sun Zhigang case was one of internal consultation. A decision of violating the Constitution was not directly made. The State Council took the initiative and withdrew the unconstitutional law.

Also, under the Chinese constitutional system, when horizontal dialogue cannot reach a unanimous result, the vertical constitutional dialogue will be brought in. According to Susan L. Shirk, one of the characteristics of the management model guided by the Chinese Communist Party is "management by exception."[38] That is, the party focuses on those important issues that cannot be resolved through routine methods of management. Under the routine management model, if two organizations with no subordinate relationship cannot reach a consensus on constitutional issues, their dialogue will continue under the guidance of a higher organ. This higher organ may be a formal legal organization or an informal organization, such as an organization in the party. On the other hand, the higher department may demand that constitutional dialogue be carried out at the lower level and recommend that "the contradictions will not be passed upward," so as to maintain harmony. In comparison, if constitutional dialogue between the three US branches cannot achieve consensus, there is no coordination mechanism among them, and they can only seek further for solutions within their own departmental system. This means that one organization makes a decision and then another organization gives a response. Therefore, it is mainly a diachronic dialogue. Under the Chinese Constitutional system, the exchange could best be described as a synchronized dialogue. In the United States, differences are recognized and differences are allowed to exist. Chinese democratic centralization stresses unity, does not acknowledge differences, and tries its best to eliminate differences. In reality, however, it is not easy to reach consensus in the strict sense, so the result of this kind of dialogue is to cover up differences with abstract decisions and leave the differences for continued dialogue in the future. At the same time, problems will be left unresolved. Furthermore, the higher the level of dialogue and consultation, the more abstract the language, so that the decisions become even more ill defined. One only has to have a look at decisions made by the Chinese Communist Party Central Committee to understand this effort in seeking minimal consensus.

Endnotes

[1] Tom Ginsburg, ed., *Comparative Constitutional Design* (Cambridge University Press, 2012), 160.

[2] A quote from Fei Xiaotong. Some scholars describe China's traditional society as a beehive.

[3] However, there are also scholars who use economic federalism to describe the motivation for the economic development of the past 30 years in China.

[4] Hao Tiechuan, "On Benign Violations of the Constitution," *Law Study* No. 4 (1966). But there are scholars who have questioned and criticized this. Refer to Tong Zhiwei, "We Should not Approve of 'Benign Violations of the Constitution,'" *Law Study* No. 6 (1996).

[5] James T. McHugh, *Comparative Constitutional Traditions* (New York: Peter Lang Publishing, 2002), 36.

[6] Remarks made to Stephan Korosec, June 12, 1987.

[7] McHugh, *Comparative Constitutional Traditions*, 33.

[8] Yin Xiaohu, "On Policy-Type Constitutional Amendments," *Legal and Commercial Studies*, vol. 1 (2000).

[9] Donald C. Clarke, "Puzzling Observations in Chinese Law: When Is a Riddle Just a Mistake?," in *Understanding China's Legal System*, ed. C. Stephen Hsu (New York: New York University Press, 2003), 93-121; McHugh, *Comparative Constitutional Traditions*, 69.

[10] Clarke, "Puzzling Observations in Chinese Law: When Is a Riddle Just a Mistake?"

[11] McHugh, *Comparative Constitutional Traditions*, 70.

[12] Mao Zedong, *Constitutional Government in the New Democracy*.

[13] Joseph Stalin, "On the Report on the 'Draft Constitution of the Soviet Union'" (1936).

[14] Zhang Youyu, *Constitution and Constitutional Government* (1940).

[15] Hu Sheng, who was the group leader of the Central Communist Party Constitution Working Group at the time, pointed out: "Rely on the whole country's organizations to guarantee the implementation of the Constitution: first the People's Congress and the Standing Committee of People's Congress, and then the whole of judicial organs, supervising organs, administrative organs and the people of the whole country. This then is the entire system for guaranteeing the implementation of the Constitution." Liu Zheng, *The Historical Footprints of the System of the People's Congress* (Chinese Democratic Legal System Publisher, 2008), 236.

[16] McHugh, *Comparative Constitutional Traditions*, 66.

[17] "Bureau of State Land Management Reply with Reference to Issues of Ownership of, and the Right to Use City Residential Sites," *State Land* (Laws and Regulations), No. 13 (April 23, 1990).

[18] This is the important reason why the judicial investigation system for administrative actions is not effective in China.

[19] Refer to the seventh article of the "Supreme People's Court in reference to the rules on judgment documents quoting standard legal documents such as laws, regulations, etc." However, there is no consensus among legal organizations regarding situations where there is a conflict with a higher level law, as to whether it definitely "cannot be applied." Refer to: Legislative Affairs Commission of the SCNPC, *Answers to Legal Questions, 2000-2005* (Chinese Democratic Legal System Publisher, 2006), 10.

[20] Xu Chongde, *History of the Constitution of the People's Republic of China* (Fujian People's Publisher, 2003), 168.

[21] Xu, *History of the Constitution of the People's Republic of China,* 169.

[22] Andrew Jackson points out that legislative organs, administrative organs, and the courts all have power to interpret the meaning of the Constitution. When every government official swears to be loyal to the Constitution, he or she must understand the meaning of the Constitution from his or her point of view. Cited from Keith E. Whittington, "The Construction of Constitutional Regimes," in *Political Foundations of Judicial Supremacy: The Presidency, the Supreme Court, and Constitutional Leadership in U.S. History,* (Princeton University Press, 2007).

[23] Kenneth G. Lieberthal, "The 'Fragmented Authoritarianism' Model and Its Limitations," in *Bureaucracy, Politics and Decision Making in Post-Mao China*, eds. Kenneth G. Lieberthal and David M. Lampton (Berkeley: University of California Press, 1992).

[24] Therefore, Peng Zhen pointed out in a meeting of the People's Congress: "The various levels of Standing Committees in the People's Congress must actively establish close connections with the party committee at the same level of government," and must "rely on the leadership of the Party and have close coordination with others, so as to function well." Peng Zhen, *On Socialist Democracy and Construction of the Legal System in the New Era* (Central Documents Publishing House, 1989), 296.

[25] Randall Peerenboom, *China's Long March toward Rule of Law* (Cambridge University Press, 2002), 46.

[26] Peerenboom, *China's Long March toward Rule of Law*, 179.

[27] Barrett L. McCormick and David Kelly, "The Limits of Anti-Liberalism," *Journal of Asian Studies*, vol. 53, no. 3 (August 1994): 804-831.

[28] Neal Devins and Louis Fisher, *The Democratic Constitution* (Oxford University Press, 2004), 45.

[29] *State Land* (Laws and Regulations) No. 13 (April 23, 1990).

[30] Devins and Fisher, *The Democratic Constitution*, 29.

[31] Philip B. Kurland, "American Systems of Laws and Constitutions," in *American Civilization* (London: Thames and Hudson, 1972), 127-148.

[32] Some scholars call it constitutional construction to differentiate it from the usual jurisprudential interpretation of the Constitution. Unlike jurisprudential interpretation, construction provides for an element of creativity in construing constitutional meaning. Keith E. Whittington, *Constitutional Construction: Divided Powers and Constitutional Meaning* (Cambridge, MA: Harvard University Press, 1999), 5.

[33] Devins and Fisher, *The Democratic Constitution*, 106.

[34] Louis Fisher, "Constitutional Interpretation by Members of Congress," 63 *North Carolina Law Review*, 707-747 (1985).

[35] Devins and Fisher, *The Democratic Constitution*, 44.

[36] Aside from the federal constitutional dialogue mechanism, there are formal and informal dialogue mechanisms between the governmental organizations of the states. Shirley S. Abrahamson and Robert L. Hughes, "Shall We Dance? Steps for Legislators and Judges in Statutory Interpretation," 75 *Minn. L. Rev.* 1045 (1991).

[37] Peng, *On Socialist Democracy and Construction of the Legal System in the New Era*, 268.

[38] Susan L. Shirk, "The Chinese Political System and the Political Strategy of Economic Reform," in *Bureaucracy, Politics, and Decision Making in Post-Mao China*, eds. Kenneth G. Lieberthal and David M. Lampton (Berkeley: University of California Press, 1992).

Zhai Guoqiang is deputy director of the Department of Constitutional and Administrative Law, Institute of Law, at the Chinese Academy of Social Sciences. He also serves as deputy secretary-general of the Chinese Association of Constitutional Law and as vice-chair of the Beijing Legislative Research Association. His research interests include constitutional theory, comparative law, and human rights.

# 2

No Deaf Left Behind

by
Leonardo Neves Correa

"Education for Inclusion" was the name of one of the courses I took as an undergraduate. Its focus was on the learning processes of students with special educational needs. And it covered a wide range of needs. The one that caught my attention was education for the deaf, who daily faced language barriers when interacting with the broader "hearing" community.

In a study on deaf pedagogy, the Byelorussian psychologist and educator Lev Vygotsky suggests that, biologically speaking, a deaf animal tends to have fewer adaptation difficulties than a blind animal does. However, the author argues that the same does not apply to humans. More than a biological handicap, deafness is, for humans, a social handicap, because it limits the individual's access to language and therefore his or her participation in society in a broader context. Studies indicate that most of the deaf population has a lower literacy level than does the hearing population. About 75 percent of deaf people in Brazil do not complete elementary education and deaf persons in higher education courses have great difficulty with written language. Studies from Gallaudet University in the United States also show that the literacy level of 18- to 20-year-old deaf students is equivalent to that of 9-year-old hearing students.

The issue of deaf literacy leads to a controversial question in education: what is the best approach for teaching the deaf? For years there has been no definitive answer to this question—and we might never have a single answer. Historically, two methods have dominated the field of deaf education: the oral method and signing. The first assumes that for a deaf person to fully integrate into the larger society, he or she needs to learn to communicate orally, and master the skills of reading and writing. The manual, or signing, approach understands that the "mother tongue" of all deaf people is sign language, and that becomes the basis of all learning processes. Currently we can observe the rise of hybrid methods of teaching, such as "total communication" and "bimodism," or "bilingualism." Total communication, as the name suggests, is a multicode approach, in which the deaf student learns to communicate in different ways, by using both signing and oral language. The model suggests that, whenever possible, students use them simultaneously. The bilingual method is opposed to this approach in the sense that it understands sign language and oral language as independent; thus one language does not become the means of learning the other. For bilingualists the focus on oral language learning is centered on writing and reading practices.

The issue, today, is not just about the best, but also about the most appropriate learning environment: the specialized school or the inclusive school. Specialized schools are more likely to provide better physical and educational resources for the education of deaf children, as well as providing greater interaction with other deaf students, which would facilitate their immersion in "deaf culture" and sign language acquisition. On the other hand, specialized schools may limit the student's contact with hearing society.

Inclusive schools introduce students to a heterogeneous context where they can interact with both deaf and hearing individuals, which contributes to the process of social integration. However, inclusive schools often do not have all the resources needed to offer minimal support for deaf students, which results in significantly lower academic performance compared to students in specialized schools.

In Brazil, the controversy over the education of the deaf gained media attention in 2011, when the Ministry of Education (MEC) proposed that all children with disabilities be mainstreamed in regular schools; special institutions would in this sense become support institutions. In Brasília, a group of approximately 500 participants, mostly members of advocacy agencies for the deaf and deaf culture, such as National Institute for Deaf Education (INES) and National Federation for Education and Integration of the Deaf (FENEIS), held a protest against the federal initiatives to limit the agency of special education institutions. Protesters fought for the right to study in a bilingual school that recognizes deaf culture and enables learning based on its special needs.

In the United States the question became an economic issue. In 2011, the State of New York submitted a budget proposal that would reduce the financing of 4,201 public schools (11 of them, specialized schools). Is it the duty of the state to invest in specialized schools for the deaf when these students can attend regular schools? This is the question that prompted me to draft an issue guide for use in deliberative community forums during my six-month residency at the Kettering Foundation. The foundation publishes a series of such guides, which are used by civic and educational organizations interested in addressing public issues. In this paper, I present a brief description of the process of bringing this guide together.

A First Attempt at Framing the Issue

The first months of the residency were dedicated to trying to identify the issues behind the problem of equality and accessibility of deaf people in mainstream society. I began with a review of articles published in the previous two years in the Brazilian media. *O Estadao de São Paulo* and *Folha de São Paulo*, Brazil's two biggest newspapers, and the website of the Brazilian Ministry of Education were selected as the major sources for research. Following are some examples of the most commented-upon articles published on the websites:

"Cinema Adapted for Deaf and Blind" http://www.estadao.com.br/noticias/arteelazer,ccbb-adapta-cinemas-no-rio-e-sp-parasurdos-e-cegos,642305,0.htm

"Deaf Group Protests against New Educational Policies" http://www.estadao.com.br/noticias/geral,surdos-realizam-protesto-contrapoliticadomec,721556,0.htm

"New Policy Wants Children with Disabilities in the Regular School" http://www.estadao.com.br/noticias/impresso,plano-quer-alunos-com-deficienciana-escola-regular,745165,0.htm

"The Deaf Should Be Educated in Their Mother Tongue and through It" http://www.estadao.com.br/noticias/impresso,o-surdo-deve-ser-educado-no-idiomamaterno-e-por-meio-dele,737415,0.htm

"Language: A Barrier to Deaf Inclusion" http://www.estadao.com.br/noticias/impresso,inclusao-de-surdos-esbarra-nalinguagem, 737414,0.htm

"Deaf People Organize Protest against Government" http://www.estadao.com.br/noticias/geral,surdos-realizam-protesto-contra-politicado-mec, 721556,0.htm

"Language Could Be Essential to the Learning of Numbers (for Deaf People)" http://www.estadao.com.br/noticias/vidae,linguagem-pode-ser-fundamental-noaprendizado-de-numeros-,677251,0.htm

Most of these examples, all retrieved from O *Estadão*, highlight the differences in the ongoing discussion about the different school models for the deaf. On the one hand we have specialized schools for the deaf and bilingual schools (which are not necessarily limited only to deaf people, but use sign language as the main language in most classes and disciplines from first to eighth grades) and, on the other hand, inclusive schools that promote the integration of students with and without special needs.

Research results from academic and other sources tended to reflect the same discussions. Therefore my thesis was that, for most people, the issue of equality for the deaf was the result of a problem within education and that solutions to the problem lay in changes within education itself. People have different thoughts and insights when it comes to education; what works for one, might not necessarily work for others. And in the case of deaf education the issue became more complicated when national efforts (influenced by international policies) started to standardize the educational system to accommodate everyone.

While the articles in scientific journals and newspapers seemed to reflect a polarization of views about the different educational environments for the deaf, the same was not so true of my conversations with deaf individuals, institutions, and experts on the subject. Indeed, the same issue appeared to be seen differently through the eyes of those I had the chance to speak with. Yes, most of them had a position on what would be the most appropriate school for the deaf, but most of them also acknowledged the legitimacy of individual choices. Thus, when an institution of advocacy would fight for the maintenance of a deaf school, it was not necessarily combating or running against the inclusive school. Those conversations and the later results from one of the focus groups I conducted in Brazil led me to think about renaming the issue I was trying to frame. Because I come from the educational area, I may have put too much emphasis on an educational approach. The informal conversations I had, a brief experience at Gallaudet University in Washington, DC, and results of the focus groups conducted in Londrina, Brazil, in 2012 pointed me in other possible directions.

Focus Group Research

When I decided to organize focus groups in Brazil I had three main questions in mind: What are the most difficult challenges deaf people face in their daily lives? What are the implications of the special educational policies for the deaf in Brazil? How do people see a deaf person in their community? To try to address these questions I put together two groups of people. In the first group were professionals and specialists in deaf education, a university professor, two researchers in the area of deafness, an interpreter, and a teacher of the deaf who works in a mainstream school environment. The second group was composed largely of first-year undergraduates studying to be teachers.

Group One: Experts

One participant related that, in her experience as a teacher of the deaf, one of the most recurrent, if not the most recurrent, issue she faces is prejudice from some parents against sign language. Some parents think that signing is an obstacle to the achievement of speech and therefore they do not allow their deaf children to sign. This obliges the children to try harder and take speech therapy to learn how to speak "properly." The outcome is normally the creation of a kind of subcommunication—what is called *gestuno*—a very basic kind of communication in which individuals try to come up with very basic signs, often related to basic commands, such as go to sleep, wake up, and brush your teeth, which does not allow parents to have more complex conversations with their deaf child.

Another difficulty regarding language acquisition reported in the group was the use of complex and abstract words. Because the sign language vocabulary is much more limited when compared to oral languages, some concepts of mass circulation are extremely hard to translate into sign language. One example would be the term *globalization*. Even though this term might well be unclear to a hearing child, chances are that a hearing person would have greater opportunities of being exposed to the term at some point—on TV, on the radio, or in a newspaper. Furthermore, it would be easier for a hearing person to make an association with the term by combining *global* with *-zation*. In an inclusive educational environment with both hearing and deaf students, for example, the teacher would likely have to provide ongoing explanations or clarifications to such concepts.

One other issue related to language, noted by the group, is the way thought is conceived. Because sign language is essentially visual and has a different grammar and vocabulary, it often interferes in the learning of deaf pupils, who frequently translate concepts from sign language to the spoken language word for word.

Also, schools (and society in general) do not recognize that Portuguese (or any other oral language) is not the deaf person's first language. Schools still evaluate deaf students based on their performance in Portuguese and the evaluation standards are the same as they are for hearing students (in order to be "fair" and "inclusive").

With regard to issues of accessibility in public settings, there is a disconnect between the deaf population and policymakers, participants in this focus group pointed out. Most legislators are not aware of the problems deaf people face. For the vast majority, deaf people are essentially the same as any other group with a disability. In most cases, however, deaf people do not see themselves as part of a disabled community. On the contrary, they see themselves as a minority linguistic group. One of the participants in the focus group reported that she was part of one town meeting between members of a local deaf population and a city counselor (who happened to be blind). The counselor suggested that city hall invest in initiatives like providing the deaf with disability cards so that they would be able to park in handicapped spots. The focus group participant reported that members of the deaf delegation were offended by the proposal because they didn't see themselves as a disabled class, and the one thing they actually needed the most was language accessibility. Because deaf people constitute a minority, most government-provided financial resources end up destined for other areas. There are still very few resources being invested in deaf-related issues. Furthermore, accessibility services for the deaf require very large investments. Providing a full-time interpreter in every public setting (hospitals, city hall, schools), for example, would require large amounts of money for a service that might not be used very often.

The United States is a pioneer in providing technological support to its deaf population. Services, such as relay telecommunication, are provided to all deaf populations: if you are not able to afford a special phone or any related technology the government might provide it free of charge. In Brazil the scene is somewhat different. One of the participants related that the government is now pressuring the biggest national telecommunication companies to provide such services to deaf people. But the initiative has not yet brought any result to light. The only technology deaf Brazilians have at their disposal are public phones with a keyboard—a device that does not even accommodate the needs of most deaf people, because the large majority of them have lower levels of literacy and cannot make use of them.

Participants could not find common ground when it came to the old issue of schools for the deaf vs. inclusive schools. The teacher of the deaf, who happened also to have experience in a specialized school, deplored the fact that specialized schools created a much more exclusive environment where deaf students didn't have a chance to interact with the rest of (hearing) society. Deaf children, she said, should have a chance to study in regular schools and be assisted constantly in a specialized institution, where they then would have a chance to interact with other deaf individuals. Another participant questioned this position by introducing the issue of adapting the curriculum for the deaf in a mainstreamed school. While hearing students would be able to read and work through complex texts, the deaf student would have to rely on interpreter assistance to try to achieve at the same level. In addition, the deaf student would face a disadvantage when it came to written tasks.

Because the law that made the Brazilian Sign Language officially national was only passed in 2005, national government efforts to recruit new and qualified interpreters are fairly recent, although there were quite a few qualified interpreters available.

Participants discussed the 60-hour course on Brazilian Sign Language (LIBRAS) every future teacher is required to take before graduating. The idea behind this requirement is that future teachers would be able to communicate (even if only on a basic level) with their deaf students. According to participants in the focus group, 60 hours are not anywhere near enough to help students learn a new language. Such classes would only work as a support class that would give student teachers an overview of the complexity of teaching a deaf child.

Participants seemed to believe it to be extremely important that deaf people engage with other deaf people. Sometimes, especially when the deaf child is born into a hearing family (which is what occurs in most cases), they don't have much opportunity to experience deaf culture, interact with other deaf people, and learn and develop sign language in an authentic environment (rather than just in schools for the deaf). For those kinds of experiences, advocacy associations for the deaf play an important role in every deaf person's life as gathering places where the deaf can get together, share experiences, build relationships, and have an opportunity to address different issues.

In response to the comments on the importance of advocacy associations to deaf culture, one of the participants raised a concern that some deaf associations are too extremist when it comes to deaf culture. She talked about the existence of some groups that are completely against cochlear implant surgeries in defense of sign language. She also mentioned that she was dating a deaf boy and because she was a hearing person she faced a lot of prejudice. According to her, her boyfriend's deaf friends thought he would be better off dating a deaf girl.

Group Two: Future Teachers

The purpose of assembling this second group was to learn about their views on the issue of deaf education and literacy. Unlike participants in the first group, the students had not been previously invited to participate in the focus group. They were caught by surprise in one of their linguistics classes when we asked them to participate. In total, 17 people took part in that group: one linguistics professor at the university (who allowed me to use the class for this research purpose); 15 first-year undergraduates studying to become teachers; and one member of the community who had a deaf relative and who was invited in order to give students an insight on the major challenges deaf people face in their daily lives based on her experience with her relative.

Even though students were willing to participate in the focus group, they were, initially, not clear about their stake in the problem. The issues of deaf literacy and education did not seem to resonate with the group at first. After the community member shared some of her experiences with her deaf relative, however, they began to connect with the problem. Her story made room for others to share their own stories and impressions about the issue.

Participants in this group focused on three main themes: inclusion of people with disabilities, the actions of advocacy groups and other institutions, and the issues arising over what kind of schools are best for educating the deaf.

The first problem addressed by the participants was the disconnect between so-called "typical" people and persons with disabilities. One of the participants mentioned having a brother with Down syndrome and how hard it was for people to include or accept him in the mainstream. According to the students, people tend to avoid otherness and the unknown because of fear of everything and everyone who is different. In the participants' perspective, deaf and hearing people should have a chance to mingle. That would be the only way they would acknowledge one another. One of the participants noted that her church had a special program for the deaf. The deaf would have special celebrations using Brazilian sign language. Initiatives of that sort help deaf people preserve their language and culture. Another participant pointed out that such organizations also ought to promote an opportunity for others to become more aware of the situation of deaf people, and that there should be places where hearing people would have a chance to interact with deaf people and learn about their language and culture.

Students discussed the most problematic issues a deaf person might face in their lives. They talked about cognition and literacy and seemed preoccupied by how they, as professionals, would deal with these matters. Many approaches were discussed: some argued that teachers should focus on instrumental activities, based on reading and writing abilities; others believed that maybe the use of technologies could reinforce the learning.

The last and most recurrent theme addressed by the group concerned educational settings. The question seemed to be problematic for the group in the sense that different conceptions of what would be an ideal educational model were brought to the table.

While some strongly believed that deaf persons and other people with disabilities should have their own schools, organized to deal with their limitations and potentialities, others argued that deaf people needed to be in a regular school, fostering more inclusive and integrative initiatives that would help them become more and more integrated with mainstream society.

One of the important things that came out of this second focus group was the perception of those who are not necessarily involved with deaf issues. The fact that there was not a strong connection to the theme of literacy and education for deaf individuals at first, even though the participants were all future teachers, led me to reflect on how I was naming the issue I was trying to frame. It had become clear that a title like "Education and Literacy for the Deaf" seemed too distant from the day-to-day reality of most people.

After the interviews and the focus groups, I felt the necessity to name this issue in a way that would resonate with more people. Therefore, I decided to move away from the educational perspective of the problem and enlarge the picture—dealing with the question of equality in a broader way. The result is presented in the next section.

Moving Forward

During the research process for the production of the issue guide on deaf equality I had the opportunity to connect with the National Association of the Deaf (NAD), Gallaudet University, and other deaf-related organizations in the United States. These organizations helped me by providing information on the issues deaf Americans face across the country. Throughout this process I have been keeping in touch with one lawyer from NAD, Andrew Phillips, who helped me revise the contents of the issue guide I was working on. On my visit to the NAD I introduced some issue guides produced for the National Issues Forums Institute (NIFI) to illustrate what I intended to do in naming and framing a deaf-related issue.

Phillips became interested in the type of work the Kettering Foundation and NIFI are doing with the issue guides and thought that such initiatives could encourage deaf people to become more politically active. We decided then to think about ways this work could relate to the work NAD was doing. NAD is the biggest association for deaf and hearing-impaired individuals in the US and has been active since 1880, when an international conference— the Milan Conference on Deaf Education—was convened. The purpose of the conference, which drew participants from all over the globe, was to define the best approach for teaching the deaf. By the end of the meeting, participants stipulated that every deaf pupil in the world should be educated through oralism (learning how to speak) rather than through sign language. The stated rationale was that sign language would make deaf people more lazy and encourage them not to learn the spoken language of their region. What became controversial about this decision was that most of the participants of that conference were actually hearing. There were only a few deaf representatives and sign language supporters present.

NAD was born in the heat of that moment. Its mission, in addition to supporting sign language, was to give deaf people a voice in the decision-making process related to the issues that concern them (which was the theme of the 2012 NAD conference: "Nothing about Us, Without Us!").

Leonardo Neves Correa is an adjunct professor in the Foreign Language Department at the State University of Londrina-UEL in Brazil, where he earned an undergraduate degree in modern foreign languages and a master's degree in language studies. His research interests include EFLT training, civic education, education policy, educational inclusion, and new technologies.

3

Global Trends in Agricultural Policymaking and Production*

by
Tendai Murisa

Agriculture is back. There are many reasons for the sudden resurgence of interest in agriculture, notable among them the global food crisis of 2007 and 2008, and the recent economic crisis in the Eurozone. However, before we celebrate the resurgence of land-based livelihoods, especially crop and livestock farming, we need a bit of historical context. The development of agriculture, unlike any other productive sector, has posed a major challenge for modernization theory. It was assumed that, with industrialization, small family farms would eventually be absorbed by large-scale agriculture leading to the conversion of peasantries into paid workers, either on the large farms or in urban-based manufacturing firms. However, contrary to the "disappearing peasantries" assumptions we still find that in almost every geographic region there exist pockets of small family farms of varying sizes and significance to the economy.

The share of the population living in rural areas is greater in the global South than in the developed regions but there is a remarkably growing interest around small family farm systems within both the North and the South. The development of agriculture to feed the world is, indeed, a global

---

* This essay is excerpted from a book written by the author entitled, *Agents and Agency: Rural Development and Democracy Practices Revisited.*

concern. Currently, agriculture is organized through a global network of commodity chains based on the logic of profit maximization. Despite the production efficiencies that have been realized since the 1950s, instances of increasing hunger and rural vulnerability persist, suggesting the need to rethink the current model of agricultural production.

The smallholder sector has operated under very difficult conditions, in part because of the manner in which government policies have neglected it in favor of large-scale commercial agriculture operations. It is no coincidence that in many of the developing regions smallholder systems have not benefited from the technological advancements that have taken place since the beginning of the 20th century. The discussion on the following pages focuses on the global evolution of agricultural policies since the 1940s and how these developments affected the smallholder sector in the underdeveloped regions.

The Evolution of Global Agricultural Policymaking

There are three critical phases worth discussing: the post-World War II years; the "green revolution"; and the rise of market-centered approaches to rural development. These historical landmarks set the tone for the prospects, pace, and potential for global agricultural policy reforms.

Postwar Transatlantic Deals

This was a period of competition for spheres of influence between the United States and her allies against the former Soviet Union. The stage for this competition was mostly in Asia in countries like Taiwan and South Korea. The overriding objective in this context was to preempt the need for radical land reforms in order to impose a conservative national bourgeoisie class on the land.

Immediately after the Second World War, the United States and Europe entered into an agreement for economic recovery. The postwar deal was aimed at supporting rapid reconstruction and reserving a special place for agriculture. The recovery measures for agriculture included (1) a price support system; (2) encouraging, over time, the growth of the agro-industrial complex through hybrid seed technology; and (3) exporting the model into Europe. The underlying objective of the plan was the reconstruction of dynamic economies with integrated agriculture and industries undergirded by a trade system acceptable to both the United States and European countries.

the end of the 1970s. The 1980s saw a resurgence of conservatism in terms of the operations of the market promoted by US President Ronald Reagan and British Prime Minister Margaret Thatcher. Essentially, this period was characterized by the return of thinking about the superiority of the unfettered market and nonintervention by the state into the market. The defining characteristic of the period, as far as rural development was concerned, was the introduction of the "willing seller" and "willing buyer" scheme in land reforms. The scheme was based on the principle that a land market exists or can be created in which the value of land will be maximized.

In terms of overall economic management the guiding principles promoted the liberalization of trade in every sector and macroeconomic stability. Developing countries were encouraged to effect economic reform programs, commonly known as Structural Adjustment Programs (SAPs) through the enticement of balance-of-payments support. The prescription for economic reform was standard: deregulation of national currencies and prices, and commercialization and privatization of previously state-controlled industries and public services (Fine 2000; Moyo and Yeros 2005). Agriculture suffered the most; implementing countries were advised to unilaterally withdraw all support for agriculture and to implement (land) titling programs that eventually contributed to the commodification of peasants' agricultural land.

Furthermore, implementing countries have been advised to focus on exports where they have a comparative advantage. This has led to the emergence of new export-oriented land uses, such as ostrich farming and eco-tourism (Moyo 2000), and a more pronounced emphasis on setting aside increasing amounts of land for cash crops, such as tobacco and paprika, at the expense of staple grains. These shifts have contributed to pushing more farmers into commodity production for an already saturated market. Rural areas have borne a huge cost of economic restructuring as these measures have gone far in removing state support for farm production. Furthermore, these reforms have unleashed suffocating market forces by devaluing currencies and raising the cost of production. Structural adjustment has been instrumental in the intensification of demand for land as a consequence of the generalized decline in sources of income (Moyo and Yeros 2005).

During the 1970s there had been considerable optimism surrounding the contribution of agriculture towards GDP and eventual industrialization, but that dream never materialized. Countries that were originally net food exporters had, by the late 1990s, become net importers. Currently most of the Sub-Saharan (SSA) region faces significant agrarian constraints made manifest by declining agricultural yields, an increase in food insecurity, limited uptake of technological innovations, an upward trend in rural-urban migration, and increased levels of poverty. There are various causes for this collapse but chief among them are inadequate government support to smallholders, weak penetration and uptake of technological innovations, limited use of scientifically treated hybrid seeds, and insecure land-tenure systems that continue to marginalize people, especially women.

Thus the total effect of the ten years of structural adjustment was the "lost decade" of the 1980s in Africa (Mafeje 2003). As noted above, the reforms have resulted in devaluing currencies and raising the cost of production. Other adjustment measures that weakened the potential for agricultural growth were the lowering or removal of tariffs, which meant that imports could enter freely; thus food prices are determined by the price at the border rather than by domestic agricultural production (Hazell et al. 2007). In 2009, a consortium of international NGOs, Germanwatch, BothENDS, FIAN Germany, FIAN International, and UK Food Group carried out an investigative mission on the state of smallholder agriculture in Zambia, Uganda, and Ghana. They concluded that adjustment programs had a severe negative impact on smallholder agriculture and also pointed out that EU trade policies were worsening conditions amongst the smallholders in these countries (FIAN 2009).

The 1980s were indeed a lost decade for more than one reason: (1) there was no notable land reform and where it was attempted it was at a very high price, thereby limiting possibilities of funding broader agrarian reform, (2) there was a notable decline in levels of national food security due to conversion of land use to export crops, and (3) an increase in land-based conflicts due to foreign investment induced the loss of agricultural land. Furthermore, tariff reductions have weakened the potential for agricultural growth.

The Contemporary Smallholder Agriculture Sector

Africa, in its entirety, has not yet started its agricultural revolution, without which no further stage of development can be considered. Smallholder systems have either declined in productivity or remained stagnant except with regard to export products. In its current state, smallholder agriculture

Technological and Infrastructure Issues

Contemporary challenges for the majority of smallholders include lack of access to new technologies. In countries like Tanzania, Malawi, and Uganda, farmers still use hoes to till the land. In most instances the same smallholders are trapped by the rising costs of products like seeds, depend upon human labor, and often do not have sufficient or high-quality land.

New technologies are not being generated fast enough because of limited public and private investments and global market controls. The inadequacy of investments in rural and agricultural infrastructures, such as irrigation facilities (including dams and field equipment), rural transport facilities (roads, bridges, ports, and vehicles), bulk food storage (and grain reserve) facilities, as well as ancillary services like electricity, have tended to limit the expansion of food production and marketing and thus food distribution and access. Whereas prior to economic reforms, research and development were the preserve of the state they have now been removed from the public domain and serve the interests of large-scale agriculture. In the absence of a viable alternative the dependence on costly imported fertilizers has increased.

Furthermore women's access to technological improvements, such as improved seed, fertilizers, and pesticides, is limited because national legislation and customary law do not allow them to share property rights with their husbands, or because female heads of household are excluded from land-entitlement schemes and, consequently, cannot provide the collateral required by lending institutions. They are frequently not reached by extension services and are rarely members of cooperatives, which often distribute government-subsidized agricultural products and vital market information to small farmers. In addition, they lack the cash income to purchase needed farm products even when they are subsidized.

The technological disparities between farmers in the West and those in Sub-Saharan Africa have been further exacerbated by the agricultural subsidy regimes in the world's richest countries, which together spend more than $200 billion subsidizing their own agricultural sectors—much of the aid going to benefit large-scale farmers (Weiss 2007). These same countries devote less than $1 billion a year in official development assistance to agricultural development in the developing world.

International Trade Systems and Smallholder Agriculture

Increasingly, agricultural land-use patterns have been changed to service saturated world commodity markets to the extent that approximately 40 percent of the word's total agricultural production is now traded across national borders. In 2004, both the United States and the European Union produced roughly 17 percent of the world's agro-exports by value, Canada, Australia, and New Zealand together accounted for 15 percent, and the major South American exporters (Brazil, Argentina, Chile, and Uruguay) 13 percent (Weiss 2007). This means that 62 percent of the world's agro-exports in 2004 came from 4 percent of the world's agricultural population. The large-scale nature of production in these regions has contributed to a 60 percent decline in prices of the "big three" cereals: maize, rice, and wheat. The Food and Agricultural Organization (2003) notes that "depressed [commodity] world prices create serious problems for poor farmers in developing countries who must compete in global and domestic markets with these low-priced commodities and lack safeguards against import surges."

If the situation is not adequately addressed, the destructive patterns of agricultural trade described here will deepen considerably in the coming decades, with grain and livestock exports from the major producing nations dominating the world market and rising food import dependence in much of the developing world. Compared with the late 1990s, grain imports from the developed world to the underdeveloped regions are expected to double by 2020 (Weiss 2007). These trends will inevitably make smallholder agriculture increasingly unattractive and lead to what others, such as Brycesson et al. (2003) and Weiss (2007), call the "depeasantisation" of Africa's countryside. This phenomenon is already adding to congestion in the cities without any industrialization—a pattern of migration that can be seen as one of a bundle of strategies used by the rural poor to cope with an austere environment.

Conclusion

The discussion in this essay has shown that despite the growth in agricultural production and associated scientific technologies, and despite the efforts of a number of ambitious programs intended to help—or perhaps because of them—many smallholders in rural areas of developing countries still have to contend with cyclic poverty and food insecurity. Notably missing from the corporate model of agriculture are those who lack the money needed to access commoditized food markets.

The prospects are not entirely bleak. In the midst of these disappointments there have emerged countermovements or philosophies in agricultural development, premised on a vision of achieving food sovereignty through the restructuring of global commodity chains, the prioritization of local consumption, and the sustainable utilization of land and related natural resources. Some rural communities have harnessed their civic agency into a wide range of associational forms, which include savings and loan societies, self-help organizations, multipurpose cooperatives, occupational groupings, farmers' unions, and, since the 1960s, rural-based NGOs. However, technological advances, trade-in commodities, and other innovations suggest that these local forms of isolated and autonomous organization will not be enough to meet the immense challenges. Rather, viable food systems have to take into consideration the interconnected nature and interdependencies among global communities, while emphasizing the importance of the local.

What is required is a strong, concerted push for comprehensive reforms that effectively address the constraints in agriculture (such as skewed land-ownership patterns and the inefficiencies of commodity markets) and lead to proposals for measures that critically rethink the role of the state in agrarian interventions and change. All the stakeholders, including states, NGOs, and local communities, urgently need to find ways of working together, each playing its role in implementing smallholder-focused agricultural reforms and community development. These reforms must focus on redirecting production to the local and national markets and create dynamic synergies with domestic wages, while broadening domestic demand for industrial goods and services. Such a strategy should lean towards small- and, in some instances, middle-sized farms and redirect production to the home market. It should devote more attention to enhancing collective civic action, with local consumption and demand for manufactured goods. The state also needs to develop the capacity to effect the desired policies and mobilize popular social forces in support of the vision of food sovereignty.

References

Bernstein, H. *"The Peasantry" in Global Capitalism: Who, Where and Why?* London: Merlin Press, 2000.

Biney, A. "Land Grabs: Another Scramble for Africa," *Pambazuka*, Issue 448 (2009). Available at: http://pambazuka.org/en/category/features/58809.

Bryceson, D., C. Kay, and J. Mooij, eds. *Disappearing Peasantries? Rural Labour in Africa, Asia and Latin America.* London: Intermediate Technology Publications, 2003.

Cotula, Lorenzo, Sonja Vermeulen, Rebeca Leonard, and James Keeley. *Land Grab or Development Opportunity? Agricultural Investment and International Land Deals in Africa.* London/Rome: IIED/FAO/IFAD, 2009.

FIAN. "Policies to Overcome the Marginalisation of African Peasant Farmers." *Policy Implications of Project Work on African Smallholders in Focus and Voice in EU Trade Policy.* December 2009.

Fine, B. *Social Capital versus Social Theory: Political Economy and Social Science at the Turn of the Millennium.* London and New York, 2000.

Hazell, P., C. Poulton, S. Wiggins, and A. Dorward. *The Future of the Small Farms for Poverty Reduction and Growth 2020 Vision.* Discussion Paper 42. Washington DC: IFPRI, 2007.

Helliker, K. D. "A Sociological Analysis of Intermediary Non-Governmental Organizations and Land Reform in Contemporary Zimbabwe," DPhil. Thesis, Rhodes University, 2006.

Long, N. *Development Sociology: Actor Perspectives.* London: Routledge, 2001.

Mafeje, A. "The Agrarian Question, Access to Land and Peasant Responses in Sub-Saharan Africa, Civil Society and Social Movements Programme," Paper No. 6, Geneva: UNRISD, 2003.

Moyo, S. *Land Reform under Structural Adjustment in Zimbabwe: Land Use Change in the Mashonaland Provinces.* Uppsala: Nordiska Afrika Institutet, 2000.

Moyo, S. and P. Yeros, eds. *Reclaiming the Land: The Resurgence of Rural Movements in Africa, Asia and Latin America.* London: ZED Books, 2005.

Pollock, R. "Egypt Leases Land in Uganda to Ensure Food Security." February 4, 2010. Accessed March 26, 2015. http://allafrica.com/stories/201002040892.html.

Sharife, K. "Land Grabs: Africa's New 'Resource Curse.'" *Pambazuka News* (October 26, 2009). Accessed March 26, 2015. http://pambazuka.net/en/category.php/features 60526.

Thompson, Carol. *Agrofuels from Africa, not for Africa.* Routledge Press, 2008.

Weiss, T. *The Global Food Economy: The Battle for the Future of Farming.* Zed Books, London, 2007.

Tendai Murisa is the executive director of TrustAfrica, an African-led foundation focused on securing conditions for democratic governance and equitable development throughout the continent. To date, his research and writings have been focused on rural development, agency, and democracy with the aim of helping to empower communities to determine their own futures. Murisa has published a number of peer-reviewed journal articles and book chapters and has co-edited three books.

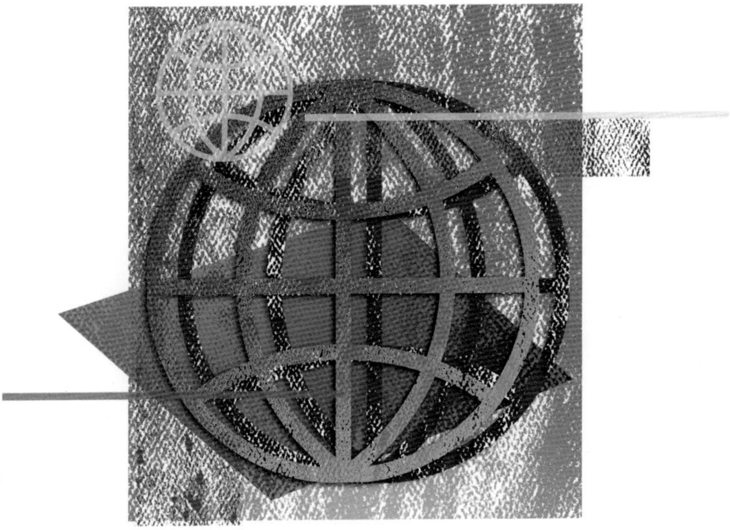

4

An Analysis of Ideological Factors in the Selection Process for Justices of the Supreme Court in the United States

by
Liu Hui

Supreme Court justices play an important role in the political life of the United States. Selection of the justices is an important component of American political life and an important focus of academic research. Research published by Henry Abraham has had an immense influence. He has proposed six factors which influence the selection of the justices: "obvious judicial quality; professional skills and abilities; absolute integrity in personal and professional character; a quick, active and clear mind; . . . professional training or similar education; and clear written and oral communicative ability."[1] Believing that judicial ability is the main factor influencing the selection process of the justices, many people accept to a certain degree the myth that selection of justices means selection of the good and able for the office. However, studies by Keith E. Whittington and David M. O'Brien show that, in reality, the selection of a justice "must weigh the support or opposition forces of Congress and the White House, and must satisfy the representational demands of geography, religion, race, sex, ethnic group and others,"[2] making it almost a purely political appointment. The pioneering studies of Whittington and O'Brien were followed by a great number of explorations based on legal theory and the political system. This article focuses on analyzing the ideological[3] factors that affect the selection process of the justices; it discusses the influence of ideological factors on the president, political parties, interest groups, and the Senate in the selection of the justices.

The Ideological Background

In the United States, the ideology of liberalism strongly influences the whole process of justice selection for the Supreme Court. The classical ideology of liberalism embraces democracy, individual liberty, and the conviction that the main purpose of government is to protect individual rights. It opposes state intervention and advocates unrestrained freedom. This plays an important role in supplying the legal basis for politics, solidifying social forces, judging the value of social activities, raising the level of social psychology, supplying direction and pathways, and influencing the lifestyles of most members of society. One of its most important functions is to provide a social atmosphere through political means to direct citizens' understanding of self-interest, thereby legalizing the political process. Historically, as the goal of "seeking a better life" on the part of early European immigrants to North America continuously conflicted with the interests of Great Britain, ideology played an important role in lending legitimacy to the separatist movements that arose from the uneven division of gains, and in the design of the political system after the founding of the country.[4]

Before the War of Independence, the conflict of interests between the North American colonies and Great Britain centered on the political status of the colonies and their immigrants vis-a-vis the mother country. After independence, however, the conflict centered on distribution of rights among the federal, state, and local governments and the citizens.[5] During the Revolution, the immigrants employed the social-contract theory of "no taxation without representation" as the legal weapon to declare war on Great Britain, thus using war to solve the conflict of interests between the colonies and their mother country. After the revolution, the new nation, which was facing problems both from within and without, adopted John Locke's idea of "limited government," and applied Montesquieu's theory of "separation of the three powers" in the design of their political system. Horizontally, it separates the executive, the legislative, and the judicial branches of government with checks and balances. Vertically, it regulates the division of power between the federal and state governments.

Two insights may be derived from gaining an understanding of the above-mentioned legalization of political process through the ideology of liberalism. First, without exception, the rule of law became a component of the ideology of liberalism, which legalized the political process of the separatist movement and the system of checks and balances. Second, politics is the sum total of various types of activities implemented by various interest groups for gaining, retaining, and seizing power.[6]

Judicial power was set up to be relatively independent in the system of checks and balances, with the justices given the appearance of detached arbitrators with the authority to interpret the Constitution through court decisions that would impact the political process. This then forced participants to obtain the power to interpret the Constitution by influencing the process of justice selection, thereby promoting their own ideology to a dominant status to serve politics. Thus ideological factors have strongly influenced the selection process of the justices.

In the 1930s, through the reforms by the Democrats under Franklin D. Roosevelt, after the classical ideology of liberalism had accepted Keynesian economics and the goal of a welfare state, classical liberalism came to be called conservatism. Before this, the emphasis of ideological factors influencing the process of the selection of justices took the form of competition between different powers on the spectrum within classical liberalism. After this, however, the spectrum of liberalism swayed between conservatism and liberalism. The struggle over political direction was decided by the maneuvering of checks and balances, and the scope of the swing of the ideological spectrum was bounded by the limits of what would be acceptable to other groups. They held to the logic that the freedom sought by liberalism is freedom that can be freely conserved, and the conservatism sought by conservatives is conservatism that conserves freedom.[7] The selection process for justices came to embody ideological value orientations and historical specifics as well as constantly changing power balances and political game-playing outcomes.

The historical contents of ideology determine the value orientations of the selection process. From the establishment of the new country to the conclusion of the Civil War, competition on the spectrum of classical liberalism was shown in the struggles over the distribution of power between the state and federal governments. The federalists chose John Marshall as a justice because he "completely agreed with the federalists to establish a swung even farther toward conservatism. In the 2004 election, the younger Bush abandoned the policy of winning swing voters and directly embraced the Gospel faction, declaring an all-out war on liberalism in the areas of religion, abortion, homosexuality, and gun control. Winning the election through abandoning swing voters is a powerful footnote to the fact that the United States took a major step towards the ideology of a "right-wing empire." And in the 2000 general election, when the Supreme Court decisively sent the younger Bush to the White House, we see a typical example of how ideology impacts the political direction of the Supreme Court. However, with the setbacks imposed on neo-conservatism, the ideological spectrum began to move leftwards, to the extent that there appeared to be voting blocs of three conservatives, four liberals, and two swing voters, one tending right and one, left.[11] The Supreme Court again showed a tendency toward liberalism.

After the Roberts court was established in 2005, Chief Justice Roberts, under the rubric of promoting a neutral "judicial minimalism," united the conservative justices in gradually overturning the precedents that originated under the liberal justices. In abortion, religion, and gun-control agendas, the Supreme Court again leaned to the right between 2006 and 2008.

President Obama, who took office in 2008, has fully displayed the liberal ideology in the social and cultural arenas. He has explicitly showed support for abortion and the judgment of *Roe v. Wade*. Furthermore, he nominated Sonia Sotomayor in May 2009 and Elena Kagan in 2010 to be justices. It is not likely that conservative justices Roberts, Alito, and Scalia will leave the Supreme Court soon. All Obama can do is prevent the Supreme Court from continually leaning to the right, but he cannot make it turn left. So we can see that the strength of the ideological swings profoundly impacts the selection of the justices and the political direction of the Supreme Court, and, through the judicial judgment, will strengthen or weaken existing ideologies.

The political system of checks and balances offers the possibility and necessity for the effectiveness of ideological factors in the selection and appointment of the justices. The actual operation of the two-party system, the separation of powers, federalism, and the legislative power of the Senate and House of Representatives has kept American interest groups from forming a political monopoly in legislative, judicial, and administrative areas. However, seizing upon the right to explain the Constitution to uphold vested interests through the selection and appointment of justices has created the possibility for ideological factors to be effective in the process of selecting and appointing the justices. Since the establishment of the country, justices of the Supreme Court have made important decisions that have affected the course of the country's social development on power distribution between state and federal governments, slavery (1789-1861), upholding the laissez-faire market economy (1861-1937), and safeguarding and expanding civil rights (1937-2011) in cases like *Dartmouth College v. Woodward*,[12] *Scott*,[13] *Slaughterhouse*,[14] and *Roe v. Wade*. Thus, the "president with no reason not to pack the court—[appoints] those who endorse his political and philosophical principles, to the Supreme Court."[15] The so-called "unreviewability of political issues" is the bottom line for the possibility and necessity offered by the checks and balances system for ideological factors to come into play in the process of selecting justices. *Marbury v. Madison* firmly established the power of "the Supreme Court ... to review the laws made by Congress and by the states as well as decisions made by the President."[16] Since then, the Supreme Court has made use of its independent power to choose whether to accept and hear cases, and its legal right to the flexible use of precedents in making judgments with constitutional significance in dealing with civil rights, the rights of criminal defendants, and the rights of the accused to enjoy due process by the police. All of these result in their carefully making use of the option of whether to hear a case so as to avoid political disputes.[17] The justices have always opted to avoid substantial contradictions when dealing with litigation that involves specific political issues, allowing them to be resolved by formulaic procedures. For example, in *Marbury v. Madison*, which firmly established the judicial review power of the Supreme Court, Chief Justice Marshall avoided responsibility for solving the specific problem by finding that the plaintiff's appeal was not within the jurisdiction of the Supreme Court. In *Roe v. Wade*, a proviso that abortion would harm a woman's health was appended so as to perfunctorily meet the demands of the conservative forces. Even in the adjudication of the national election dispute, the content actually focused on the issue of procedure—that is, ballot counting—covering up the real political issue with procedural adjudication. In the highly political *Scott* case, the Supreme Court decided to maintain the slavery status of escaped slaves with the procedural argument that the court for the first trial did not apply the correct law. However, because it was unable to avoid political conflict, it fueled the outbreak of the Civil War, and was termed as an "extraordinarily foolish act."[18]

As we have seen, the Supreme Court has extremely limited ability to solve political disputes. Only by persisting with the bottom line of the "unreviewability of political matters," that is to say, only within the permissible scope allowed by the checks and balances system can the court's decisions be accepted by the society. Otherwise, it would lead to social unrest. This makes the presidents, senators, and their parties who represent various interest groups, veto or abandon extreme nominees and do their utmost to send those who share their own ideologies to the Supreme Court.

Ideology legalized the design of the political system of checks and balances and supplied directions and pathways for it, stimulating political participants to compete for influence in the process of selecting justices. Its historical content decides the value orientation of justice selection. The intensity of the swing within its spectrum profoundly influences the political direction of the Supreme Court. At the same time, it is constrained by the degree of tolerance of other interest groups, and is revealed in issues like partisan division, presidential nomination, senate confirmation, and interest-group promotion.

The Ideological Factors of Partisan Division

The ideological factors of partisan division in the selection and appointment of justices are mainly reflected in the party affiliation of the candidates and the power of the senate majority to control the process. First, the clear distinctions of narrow partisanship become the basic rule that determines ideological alignment. The US Constitution does not stipulate any political party system. However, it is an indisputable fact that, within the system of checks and balances, the political parties representing different interest groups compete for the right to govern and to act, "to the extent that parties are considered the foundation of the constitutional system." Recommending their own party members to be chief justice has been the consistent practice for all parties since the establishment of the Supreme Court. According to the statistics showing party affiliation of the justices from 1789 to 2011, more than 90 percent of the 112 appointed justices belong to the same party as the president. In most cases, when the justices were nominated and confirmed, the Senate was dominated by the same party as the president. During George Washington's presidency, the first to fourth Houses and Senates were controlled by the administrative branches and Federalists who supported the president. The three chief justices and eight justices appointed were all Federalists from the executive branch. John Adam's presidency extended through the fifth and sixth Senates. The fifth Senate was controlled by the Federalists, so he made use of it and appointed one chief justice and two justices of his own party. During the Democratic-Republican presidencies of Thomas Jefferson, James Madison, and James Monroe, the same party controlled the majority of seats from the 7th to the 18th Houses and Senates, and 6 Democratic-Republican justices occupied Supreme Court seats. During the terms of the Democrats Andrew Jackson, Martin Van Buren, James Knox Polk, Franklin Pierce, James McGill Buchanan, Thomas Woodrow Wilson, Franklin Delano Roosevelt, Harry S. Truman, John F. Kennedy, Lyndon Johnson, Bill Clinton, and Barack Obama, the Democratic Party respectively controlled majority seats of the 21st-26th, 29th-30th, 33rd-36th, 49th-50th, 63rd-65th, 73rd-82nd, 87th-90th, 103rd, and 110th Houses and Senates, so they appointed 34 justices and 4 chief justices of their own party. During the term of President John Taylor of the Whig Party, the majority seats of the 28th House and Senate were of his own party and he appointed one chief justice. During the terms of Republican presidents Abraham Lincoln, Ulysses Simpson Grant, Rutherford Birchard Hayes, James Garfield, Benjamin Harrison, William McKinley, Theodore Roosevelt, William Taft, Warren Harding, Calvin Coolidge, Herbert Hoover, Dwight Eisenhower, Richard Nixon, Gerald Ford, Ronald Reagan, George Herbert Walker Bush, and George Walker Bush, the Republicans had the majority seats of the 37th-48th, 51st-52nd, 55th-62nd, 67th-72nd, 83rd-86th, 91st-94th, 97th-102nd, and 108th-109th House and Senates, and they appointed 42 justices and 10 chief justices of their own party. Clearly, the historical record of appointments to the Supreme Court is a true reflection of partisanship.

Furthermore, historical changes in ideological content become increasingly varied and this affects the power of the Senate majority party controlling the selection and appointment process of the justices. The above facts show that partisanship represents the inevitability of the ideological factor phenomenon. This, does not, however, explain the complex ideological connotations reflected in many political aspects of the party factor. For example, why when the same party controls the Senate and the presidency, is there still uncertainty about whether it can control the process of appointing justices? History has shown that changes in the degree of complexity of ideological content change the power of the Senate majority party to control the process. Before the New Deal, the ideological content is fairly simple and the Senate majority party has considerable power in controlling the process. After the New Deal, the ideological content becomes increasingly diversified and the power of the Senate majority party to control the selection and appointment of justices becomes weaker. The different choices in matters concerning justices by the Federalists in 1800 and by the Democratic Party in 1937 offer a vivid illustration.

When John Adams was in power, the United States was still an agrarian society whose social structure was relatively simple and there were fewer interest groups. The election system excluded many people, and the ideological spectrum, which governed the Senate majority party, was relatively simple and uniform. At the same time, "the large number of political parties established in the 19th century, was partly to prove the correctness of principles and people were surprised to find that they could conduct matters based on those principles"[19] and this caused party members to develop a strong party spirit. When the Democratic-Republican Party won the 1800 election and took control of the Senate, Adams, taking advantage of the opportunity while the Federalists still held the Senate, nominated Secretary of State John Marshall to be chief justice of the Supreme Court. Even though Federalists in the Senate had objections, they yielded to President Adams' strong request and approved the appointment in order to eliminate the chance for the incoming president—Democratic-Republican Thomas Jefferson—to appoint a chief justice, Immediately thereafter, the Federalists passed the "1801 Judicial Law," which changed the number of justices from six to five, in order to prevent judicial deadlock. And this eliminated any chance for Jefferson to appoint a justice.

When Roosevelt was in power, the United States was already a world power. The structure of social benefits became highly complex. Interest groups, such as women and workers, who had been largely excluded from elected office, were brought into the political process. Classical liberal ideology was changed to modern liberalism, which accepted state intervention and the goals of a welfare state. As ideological content became increasingly richer the demand for hewing to party interests became more decentralized, the party spirit of members declined, and the power of the Senate majority party to control the selection of justices became much weaker. To seek election, majority party members had to appease greatly inflated numbers and types of voters and therefore the majority party was unable to monopolize election resources. During the 19th century, party support could be received only if party members observed party discipline; otherwise they would be "reduced to a small faction with no weight."[20] This threat no longer held sway. Senators who sought reelection had to first cater to the needs of their voters, and only then consider the interests of their party.[21] Because 12 new laws had been voted down by the conservative Supreme Court, during his first term, Democratic President Franklin Roosevelt, after winning his second term in 1936, immediately activated a plan to pack the Supreme Court. He proposed that if a federal judge had not retired within six months of turning 70, the president could appoint a new judge to that court. The number of the justices of the Supreme Court was increased from 9 to 15. At this time, the Democratic Party controlled both Congress and the presidency, but the president's plan to pack the court suffered a serious setback. In March 1937, Congress could only pass the "law of the Supreme Court retirement system," which stipulated the retirement of the justices.

Partisanship is the basic rule in the impact of ideological factors on the context of partisan division in the selection process of the justices. And the differences in the interests of the parties and their members decide the differences in positions on the ideological spectrum; they adjust their own political needs to the swings of the ideological spectrum. Faced with the fact that the structure of social interests and ideological substances is becoming ever more complex, the ideological factors in the party controlling the selection process of justices will necessarily encounter more differences, increasing the areas of intraparty struggle. Thus the power of the Senate majority party to impact the selection process of justices is showing a tendency to decline.

Ideological Factors Related to the President

According to the Constitution, candidates for Supreme Court justice are nominated by the president, and then appointed after confirmation by the Senate. The president plays a key role in the selection of the justices. The following two aspects reveal that ideological factors have important, but not absolute, effects on the nomination process of justices by the president.

First, the president's personal ideology is of utmost importance. When the president nominates a candidate for justice, the scope of ideological considerations is not limited to partisan division. He must try hard to raise his own ideology to a dominant position and to continue to do so through his choice of justices throughout his term(s) of office. Since 1789, more than 90 percent of the appointed justices have been of the same party as the president; during this time, the same party has also controlled the Senate. This makes the ideological aspects of partisan division and the ideological aspects of the presidential nomination highly consistent. However, there have been some exceptions: 13 justices of the 112, and 2 chief justices among the 18, have been chosen across party lines. Historically, President Franklin Roosevelt appointed Republican Harlan Fiske Stone as chief justice; Truman appointed Republican Harold Burton; President Lincoln appointed Democrat Stephen Field; President Harrison appointed Democrat Howell Jackson; President Harding appointed Democrat Pierce Butler; President Eisenhower appointed Democrat William J. Brennan; President Nixon appointed Democrat Lewis F. Powell Jr.; and President Taft appointed six chief justices of whom three were Democrats (Horace Lurton, Edward White, and Joseph Lamar). Theodore Roosevelt explained this phenomenon of appointing across party lines as elevating the interests of the country over the interests of the party; presidents should make appointments based on merit, addressing "realpolitik" through the nominee.[22] However, as will be seen, the so-called realpolitik is synonymous with "harmonious coexistence of ideologies." It is a special manifestation of the function of presidential ideology under the political system of checks and balances.

Among the many cases of presidents nominating justices across party lines, Woodrow Wilson was the one who had the strongest ideological characteristics. He very much hoped "to challenge and reform the dominant position of the constitutional order through judicial organs—let the aspirations of progressivism take root and germinate in the Supreme Court."[23] In the context of Democratic Party control of both the presidency and the Senate, for his first nomination of a justice, he chose James McReynolds, a former anti-trust official in the Republican administration and then-attorney general, whom he did not know well. Wilson had highly praised James McReynolds for his achievements in anti-trust, his good reputation as a Progressive as well as his legal accomplishments, hoping he could push forward the Progressive doctrine in the relatively independent environment of the Supreme Court. It can be seen that ideological uniformity between Wilson and James McReynolds served to weaken the boundary between parties. For the same reason, when Wilson had a third opportunity to nominate a justice, he believed that John Clarke "can make free and enlightened legal interpretations" as a justice. He completely ignored the fact that although Clarke belonged to the same party as the president, it was well-known in Ohio that his party stance was not stable.

Similarly, moderate Republican President Dwight Eisenhower appointed Potter Stewart during his second term. The main reason was that the Republican Stewart supported the judgment of the *Brown* case and advocated abolishing racial segregation in education and public places. This coincided with Eisenhower's support for the unfolding Civil Rights Movement. After Eisenhower's two-term presidency, the majority of justices in the New Deal court were replaced. Although to the outside observers it would appear that middle-of-the-roader John Marshall Harlan, who was closest to the Eisenhower standard for justices in the Warren court, and Stewart were more like conservatives, "none of the Justices appointed by Eisenhower was more conservative than those they replaced."[24] Viewed objectively, Eisenhower did push the Supreme Court in a more liberal direction than the New Deal court.

From another angle, the feelings of gratitude or enmity between presidents and justices confirm the function of ideological factors in the nominations by the president. Undoubtedly ideological factors were important. However, in many cases after justices were appointed, they turned in the opposite direction of the president's wishes. Justice Salmon P. Chase, who was appointed by Lincoln, complied with the president's wishes when he was Secretary of Treasury and drew up the law to use paper currency to pay the debts incurred during the Civil War. However, when he became a justice, he expressed completely opposite opinions during the first and second cases of legal tender. Another justice explained this lightheartedly, saying: "The problems I face now are different from before."[25] In the letter Truman wrote to Justice William Douglas, he complained: "How can a Supreme Court consisting of so-called Liberals render a judgment like the case of 'taking control of the Iron and Steel Companies'?" When Justice Tom Clark, whom he nominated, was mentioned, the president did not mince words: "At first I appointed that idiot from Texas as Attorney General, and then I sent him to the Supreme Court. I have no idea what was wrong with my brain. He is not at all qualified to be Attorney General or to be in the Supreme Court. . . . It doesn't seem possible, but he is really doing badly. I think

Ideological Factors in Interest-Group Promotion

Interest groups are the social foundation of the political system of checks and balances in the United States. Ever since the establishment of the Supreme Court, interest groups have profoundly influenced the selection process of the justices. Relying on the rules of the checks and balances system and the pressures of lobbying, interest groups have exerted extensive ideological impact on the selection process of justices.

The rules of the checks and balances system are the foundation of the functioning of ideological factors for interest groups. As a systemic legal safeguard for group interests, the selection of the justices always needs to balance region, race, religion, and other characteristics of candidates.[33] Among these, selecting justices based on the circuit-riding system became key to the legitimacy of the early Supreme Court and the institutionalized rule to safeguard the interests of Southern slave owners before the Civil War. After the Civil War, Republicans intended to place Northerners in the justice positions previously occupied by Southerners, and this was supported by Northern Democrats. Southern Democrats who represented racists, on the other hand, urgently needed to combat this tactic in order to block the expansion of civil rights for blacks. After Justice William Woods retired in 1887, Democrat President Grover Cleveland, who held a distinctly racist ideology, used the excuse of balancing regional factors to nominate Lucius Lamar to replace Woods as a justice. Lamar had held positions in the Confederate government and army. Politically, while advocating division of the country, he pretended to be a reconciler in federal politics after the Civil War. Lamar's predecessor, William Woods, was from Ohio and became an army major general of the Union army after the war. Clearly, the nomination of Lamar was Cleveland's ideological choice, with the excuse of balancing regional factors, to please the racist interest groups represented by Southern Democrat conservatives. With the lowest possible support from Northern senators, Cleveland barely received enough votes to gain confirmation of his nominee.

On the surface, the reason Cleveland could obtain this result was that the racist powers used Cleveland's tariff reduction as an exchange, successfully forcing Republican senators and Democratic Northern senators to give in. But the real reason was because the United States of the 19th century was one where "black and white were clearly distinguished." The 14th Amendment stipulates the constitutional principle of prohibiting racial discrimination. However, deep-seated racist ideology dominated the political life of the whole country. There was no qualitative difference between the Democratic Party and the Republican Party in their disinclination to endow blacks with complete civil rights. President Cleveland himself opposed mixing blacks and whites in the same schools. At a press conference in 1887, he even said: "According to specialists, dividing schools is more beneficial to blacks." And when faced with the topic of tariffs, which concerned industrial and commercial groups, Republican and Northern Democrat senators definitely would not fight over racist ideology that did not concern them. After this nomination, Cleveland nominated Southerner Melville Fuller, an anti-war Copperhead from Illinois during the Civil War, as a justice and his nomination passed with significant majority confirmation. The nomination of two racists fully revealed the profound influence of racist interest groups and their ideology regarding the selection of justices. But, no matter how racist ideology influenced the process of selecting justices, regional considerations were still the dominant factor.

After the circuit-riding system was abolished in 1891, the legitimacy of the regional factor was weakened, but Cleveland continued to use it in subsequent nominations. At this time, the connotations of the regional factor exhibited even more prominently the Gilded Age ideology—that of social trends reflected in political booty and of respecting the privilege of senators. At the end of the 19th century, privileged priority in appointing administrative positions became the target of dividing the spoils between the president and the senators. Senators, especially those who came from regions where industry and commerce were flourishing, and on behalf of financial groups, challenged the president's right to appoint federal positions in the senators' electoral districts.[34] The position of Supreme Court justice did not escape this challenge. Justice Samuel Blatchford of New York State passed away in 1893 and, with the excuse of wanting to balance the number of justices from different regions, Cleveland came up with two names from his own New York State. Senior Senator David Heer of New York, however, regarded the nominations as an affront to the senator's appointment privilege as well as contrary to the best interests of local businesses. Personal enmity also played a role in Heer's opposition. He had succeeded Cleveland as governor of New York State and campaigned for the 1892 Democratic presidential candidacy against Cleveland. In addition,

[13] *Scott v. Sandford*, 60 US 393 (1857). See: Findlaw: http//www.findlaw.com/casecode/supreme (accessed Aug. 3, 2015).

[14] *Slaughterhouse Cases*, 83 US 36 (1873). See: Findlaw: http://www.findlaw.com/casecode/supreme.html (accessed Aug. 3, 2015).

[15] David M. O'Brien, *Storm Center*, 33.

[16] Henry R. Glick, *Courts, Politics and Justice* (New York: McGraw-Hill Book Company, 1993), 95.

[17] According to regulations (The Judicial Act of 1925), Congress granted the Supreme Court discretionary jurisdiction to request a transfer of records instead of making it mandatory to accept appeals. Following this, the justices developed a rule called the "four-vote principle": a case can only be heard and considered when at least four justices agree. Anyone who attempts to challenge the politically forbidden areas alone will be restrained by colleagues—author's note.

[18] David M. O'Brien, *Storm Center*, 305-306.

[19] Keith E. Whittington, *Political Foundations of Judicial Supremacy: The Presidency, the Supreme Court, and Constitutional Leadership in U.S. History* (Princeton: Princeton University Press, 2007), 272.

[20] Keith E. Whittington, *Political Foundations of Judicial Supremacy*, 272.

[21] Zhang Liping, *American Political Parties and the Election System*, 1st edition (Beijing: Social Sciences Publisher, August 2002), 6.

[22] Sheldon Goldman and Austin Sarat, *American Court Systems: Readings in Judicial Process and Behavior* (San Francisco: W. H. Freeman and Company, 1978), 286.

[23] Josephus Daniels, *The Wilson Era* (Chapel Hill: University of North Carolina Press, 1946), 540.

[24] Lawrence Baum, "Membership Change and Collective Voting Change in the United Sates Supreme Court," *Journal of Politics* 54 (1992): 122.

[25] *Hepbum v. Criswold*, 1870, Legal Tender Case, 1871. See: Findlaw: http://www findlaw.com/casecode/supreme.html (accessed Aug. 3, 2015).

[26] Merle Miller, *Plain Speaking: An Oral Biography of Harry S. Truman* (New York: Berkley, 1973), 225-226.

[27] David M. O'Brien, *Storm Center*, 53.

[28] David M. O'Brien, *Storm Center*, 63.

[29] Christopher Tomlins, ed. *The United States Supreme Court: The Pursuit of Justice* (Boston: New York Houghton Company, 2005), 269.

[30] American Bar Association, *Standing Committee on Federal Judiciary: What It Is and How It Works* (ABA, 1983), 144.

[31] According to Keith Whittington's explanation: "The opposing party is willing to accept a military hero with a vague party background/affiliation as a deliverer of its standards. The goal of selecting a military hero is to win the election efficiently." See Keith E. Whittington, *Political Foundations of Judicial Supremacy*, 163.

[32] William Brennan was a moderate liberal Democrat, a Catholic judge in the New Jersey Supreme Court. He was supported by authoritative legal circles and would not cause any trouble in the confirmation by the Senate that would influence the general election. The facts bore out Ike's shrewdness: in the Senate confirmation process, only one vote was cast against his nomination—Joseph McCarthy's.

[33] David M. O'Brien, *Storm Center*, 46.

[34] Wilfred E. Binkley, *President and Congress* (New York: Vintage, 1962), 187-204.

[35] Rufus Peckham's brother Weller Peckham participated in the party dispute aimed at Heer and investigated Heer's corruption case but was defeated. Rufus Peckham did not get involved.

[36] Keith E. Whittington, *Political Foundations of Judicial Supremacy*, 238.

[37] Keith E. Whittington, *Political Foundations of Judicial Supremacy*, 213.

[38] R. Kent Newmyer, *Supreme Court Justice Joseph Story* (Chapel Hill: University of North Carolina Press, 1985), 307.

[39] Mark A. Graber, "The Clintonification of American Law: Abortion, Welfare, and Liberal Constitutional Theory," *Ohio State Law Journal* 58 (1997): 731.

Liu Hui is an assistant researcher in the Political Research Division of the Institute of American Studies at the Chinese Academy of Social Sciences (CASS) in Beijing. A former editor at CASS, Liu has published a number of academic papers and articles about the United States in Chinese newspapers and magazines.

5

Can the Equal Protection Doctrine in the United States Be Applied to Judicial Practice in China?

by
Jing Zhou

Several legal cases advocating equal rights have been brought to court in China in the last few years. In July of 2003, Jiang Tao sued the Chengdu branch of the People's Bank of China at the People's Court in the Wuhu district of Chengdu in Sichuan Province for its requirement (which appeared in recruitment advertisements) that people be a certain height, a requirement that infringed upon the equal rights of state employees as set out in the Constitution. This case has been deemed "the first case of equal rights in China." In June of 2003, Zhang Jie received the highest score in the Wuhu civil service qualification examination but was rejected because he had tested positive for hepatitis B. In October, Zhang Jie sued the Wuhu Human Resources Bureau for violating his constitutional rights of equality and political participation. Later, there were other cases relating to discrimination based on gender, hepatitis B, AIDS, and geographic region. These cases not only engendered discussion of equal rights protection in academic circles but also attracted wide attention in society.

In these cases, some plaintiffs quoted clauses relating to equality in the Constitution as the basis for their rights, even claiming that some regulations or local laws and regulations violate the principle of equal rights. In fact, the Chinese Constitution and laws all have stipulations relating to equal rights. For example, the first clause of the 4th Article of the Constitution stipulates that all nationalities in China are equal; the second clause of the 32nd Article stipulates that all citizens of the People's Republic of China are equal before the law. The Employment Promotion Law also stipulates that people all enjoy an equal right to work. For example, the first clause of the 27th Article stipulates that the state guarantees that women enjoy equal rights to work as those enjoyed by men; the first clause of the 28th Article stipulates that all workers of all nationalities have equal rights to work; the first clause of the 29th Article stipulates that the country guarantees that handicapped people enjoy the right to work; the 30th Article says: "the recruiting unit must not use the reason that a candidate carries an infectious disease to refuse the person employment." The first clause of the Second Article of the Law on the Protection of Rights and Interests of Women stipulates that women enjoy the same political, economic, cultural, social, and family rights as men.

There is no lack of legal provisions protecting equal rights in China. The key is how to apply these to specific cases and how to use the laws to protect the equal rights of citizens. Owing to the lack of corresponding trial experiences and thus the guidance of precedents, and the fact that the Supreme Court has not issued judicial interpretations, the varying judgments of different courts have been quite controversial. Under such circumstances, the attention of academics naturally turns to foreign countries to learn from their more mature systems and principles. The United States is not only the chief formulator of international regulations, but its mature legal system influences other countries as well. Furthermore, some scholars think that the globalization of legal systems is, in a sense, the globalization of American law.[1] And, as far as investigations of equal protection cases are concerned, American courts have formed a rather comprehensive set of principles and methodologies. As a result, some scholars advocate introducing the American system to China. For example, He Yonghong advocates introducing the American standards of judgment into China.[2]

However, there are many differences between China and the United States—the structure of the state, limitation of court power, legal system, legal culture, and other aspects. So whether, and to what degree, American principles governing equal protection could be introduced into the Chinese legal system is a topic worthy of in-depth study. Owing to the fact that the US Supreme Court has ultimate power to interpret constitutional equal rights clauses, and because equal protection doctrine formed in trial practice is observed by courts at all levels, this article will focus on the federal Supreme Court.

Can Chinese Courts Conduct Equal Rights Reviews: Prerequisites for Application

As is widely known, the US Constitution grants legislative, administrative, and judicial power respectively to Congress, to the executive branch, and to the courts. Moreover, in the 1801 case of *Marbury v. Madison*, the Supreme Court established the court's power of judicial review and constitutional interpretation. Hence, the power to review the constitutionality of legislative and administrative actions became the power of the court. If a legislative or state action violates the 14th Amendment equal protection clause of the Constitution, the court can proclaim it unconstitutional and revoke it.

The corresponding Chinese legal system is different from that of the United States. First, according to the provisions of the Constitution, the National People's Congress and its Standing Committee interpret and monitor implementation of the Constitution. The 62nd Article of the Constitution stipulates that the National People's Congress exercises the following official powers: to amend the Constitution and to supervise the enforcement of the Constitution. Second, the power to annul laws, administrative regulations, local decrees, autonomous decrees, and special decrees is not exercised by the courts even if such legal documents violate the Constitution or higher level laws. The 67th Article of the Constitution stipulates that the Standing Committee of the National People's Congress exercises the following powers: to interpret the Constitution and supervise its enforcement; to annul administrative rules and regulations, decisions, or orders of the State Council that contravene the Constitution and the statutes; and to annul those local regulations or decisions of the organs of state power of provinces, autonomous regions, and municipalities directly under the Central Government that contravene the Constitution, the statutes, or the administrative rules and regulations. Also, according to the 88th Article of the Legislative Law, the offices that have the power to amend or cancel the laws, administrative regulations, local decree, autonomous decree, or special decree are the National People's Congress and its Standing Committee, the State Council, the People's Congress of a province, autonomous region, or municipality directly under the Central Government and its

Standing Committee, and the enabling body. That is to say, the court does not have the authority to proclaim invalid the laws, administrative regulations, local decrees, autonomous decrees, special decrees, and other legal documents. Furthermore, according to Administrative Procedural Law, the Chinese court can only review the specific administrative action, but it cannot review administrative regulations, rules, or decisions with general binding force.

However, this does not mean the court in China cannot judge whether certain actions conform to the principle of equality. In concrete terms, even though the court cannot directly declare legal documents to be in violation of the Constitution or higher level laws, the courts, as trial organs, have that authority and should apply the appropriate laws. For example, the 53rd Article of the Administrative Procedural Law stipulates that, in handling administrative cases, the People's Courts should take as references regulations formulated and announced by ministries or commissions under the State Council in accordance with the law and administrative rules and regulations, decisions, or orders of the State Council, of the People's Governments of provinces, autonomous regions, and municipalities directly under the Central Government, of the cities where the People's Governments of the province and autonomous regions are located, and larger cities defined as such by the State Council. That means that the court "does not need to apply those rules that are not completely in accordance with the law and the administrative regulations."[3] The Supreme Court's "Summary of the Forum on the Problem of Applying Legal Standards in Handling Administrative Cases" points out that when taking such regulations as references the judges should judge whether the regulations are legal and effective and should apply those legal and effective rules.[4] The main point of the Judgment of the No. 5 Guiding Case published by the Supreme People's Court in 2012, was that local government rules that set up permissions and punishments that do not agree with the statutes, will not be applicable in administrative trials by the People's Court.[5] Therefore, if a certain law, regulation, or rule conflicts with the equal rights clause of the Constitution, the court does not have to enforce this legal document and can interpret it according to the Constitution. So, the court has to judge whether a certain legal document meets with the equal rights clause of the Constitution, and determine whether to apply it, even if the court does not directly declare the result of the review.

Moreover, as stated above, not only the Constitution but also other laws such as the Employment Promotion Law and the Law on the Protection of Rights and Interests of Women set up equal rights clauses. If the plaintiff sues according to the equal rights clause, the court not only has to accept the case, but also has to determine whether the disputed action violates the clause. For example, if a government refuses to employ a teacher who has contracted AIDS, is it discrimination?

Therefore, even if they do not directly declare that certain actions violate the equal rights provision in the Constitution, Chinese courts still need to judge whether a certain law, regulation, or rule fits the equal rights clause of the Constitution or a higher level law, or whether a specific administrative action contradicts the equality stipulation of a law. In these circumstances, there does exist the possibility of applying the equal protection doctrine in the United States.

The Equal Protection Doctrine in the United States

To understand the equal protection doctrine of the United States, we have to be clear about its specific contents and the steps the Supreme Court takes. Generally speaking, the process can be divided into three steps. First, the court must determine whether the action constitutes a classification—that is, whether the action the plaintiff complains of relates to his or her membership in a class (i.e., race or gender). Next, the court must apply the review criteria which clarify whether the classification is suspect, semi-suspect, or is not suspect so as to select the standard of review—that is whether it must pass a strict scrutiny test, an intermediate scrutiny test, or merely a rational basis test (a constitutional standard used to review cases involving a nonsuspect form of discrimination that requires that its nonsuspect distinction is rationally related to a legitimate interest).[6] Finally, the court must apply the specific criterion to review the governmental purpose for classification and the rationality of the method.

Classification. To conduct an equal protection review, the court must first decide whether there is classification, that is, differential treatment. Tussman and Tenbroke have proposed the classic definition of classification: a classification is a quality, characteristic, property, relationship, or any combination of these. Whether they are possessed by an individual determines whether that individual is a member of the classification or is included in it.[7] Sometimes the classification is obvious and can be seen from the legal wording, as for example, in the 1950 case of *Sweatt vs. Painter*, which contested the refusal of the University of Texas law school to accept African American students.[8] Sometimes, however, there is no way of determining whether classification exists from the legal wording alone. At this time, the practical effects of the law must be considered. Some laws are neutral on the surface, but in reality they create the effect of discrimination, as for example when the law requires that all police officers must be taller than 5'1" and weigh more than 150 pounds. Data shows that in the United States about 87 percent of males can reach this standard, but only about 51 percent of females can reach it. Therefore, this law has a discriminatory impact on female applicants.[9] Then the question is how to prove the existence of this kind of concealed classification. The Supreme Court stated in *Washington v. Davis* (1976) that proof of discriminatory impact is insufficient, by itself, to show the existence of a racial classification. The court also held that allowing discriminatory impact to suffice in proving racial discrimination "would raise serious questions about, and perhaps invalidate, a whole range of tax, welfare, public service, regulatory, and licensing statutes that may be more burdensome to the poor and to the average black man than to the more affluent white."[10] Later, the court reaffirmed this principle in a series of cases.[11]

The court does not require the plaintiff to prove that governmental discrimination is aimed at a certain group of people. Even if there is only one person who believes that the government treats him or her differently from others who are in a similar situation, he or she will have the right to sue and the court can accept the case. That is to say, there is a claim under the equal protection clause even for discrimination against a "class of one."[12]

After confirming the existence of classification, the court still cannot conduct a review of whether the action is constitutional; it must first clarify whether the action in dispute is a state action. Only when the action is a state action can the court conduct a constitutional review. The reason for this is because the 14th Amendment equal protection clause of the US Constitution prohibits discriminatory action by the state. This actually can be traced back to the legal tradition of distrust of government and restrictions on the powers of government.

However, the equal protection clause of the Constitution does not mean that the court is completely unable to deliver punishment for private discrimination. Through legal precedents, the Supreme Court has extended state action into private areas. The most well known of these cases is *Shelley v. Kraemer* (1948). Kraemer was white; he believed that the charter set up by community residents prohibited the sale of houses to African Americans or Asians. Therefore, he maintained to the court that his neighbor could not sell the house to Shelley, an African American. This case involved a deed between private individuals, which was not a state matter, so it would appear that it was not eligible for applying the constitutional equal protection clause. However, the US Supreme Court pointed out that whereas signing a deed was a private action, the action of the Missouri Supreme Court in implementing the deed was a state action. And this action deprived Shelley of the equal rights Shelley should enjoy. As a result, the court could not enforce the provisions of the charter, because to do so would be unconstitutional.[13] The Supreme Court turned the focus of the dispute from a private action to the action of the court in enforcing the charter, thus making it possible to make the 14th Amendment applicable in this case.

However, legal precedents can extend constitutional protection of equal rights to the private domain only to a certain degree. Thus the legal basis allowing the court to implement regulatory law is a series of laws passed by Congress against nongovernmental discriminatory action, such as prohibiting hotels from practicing racial discrimination, and the 1964 Civil Rights Bill forbidding discrimination on grounds of race, gender, or national origin in employment, and prohibiting discrimination against handicapped people in the Americans with Disabilities Act. Furthermore, these congressional legislative acts received the support of the US Supreme Court. In the 1968 case of *Jones v. Alfred H. Mayer Company*, the court held that according to the 13th Amendment, Congress has the right to prohibit private discrimination.[14] From then on, the applications and functions of the "conditions for state action" have been reduced. Even if cases involving equal rights cannot apply under the 14th Amendment the court can conduct reviews based on federal, state, and even local civil rights bills. Sometimes protection of equal rights by civil rights bills in state or local law is more inclusive. For example, Massachusetts' law prohibits discrimination against homosexuals and transsexuals during recruitment procedures.

Determining the Review Criteria. After clarifying that classification exists, the applicable examination criteria must be determined. Through precedents, the US Supreme Court has established three basic criteria, which are: the strict scrutiny test, the intermediate scrutiny test, and the rational basis test. The actual applicable criteria for cases are generally determined by the type of classification and whether the classification involves fundamental rights. Classifications are divided into suspect, semi-suspect, and nonsuspect classifications and are subjected to strict scrutiny, intermediate scrutiny, or a rational basis test respectively. No matter whether the classification is suspect, when it involves basic rights, the strict scrutiny test is applied.

Determining the type of classification. To determine the applicable review criteria, the type of classification has to be determined first. That is, it must be determined whether the classification is suspect, semi-suspect, or non-suspect. If it is suspect, the strict scrutiny test is applicable; if it is classified as semi-suspect, the intermediate scrutiny test is conducted. If the classification is non-suspect, the rational basis test is applied.

Usually three aspects are considered in order to determine the type of classification and the degree of suspiciousness.[15] The first is whether the characteristics are immutable and innate. For example, race, parents' marriage status, and nation of origin are innate. Classification based on these will be more suspect.[16] Wealth and the ability to drive, for example, cannot be considered innate and immutable and classification based on these characteristics will be less suspect. Second, the question of whether a specific group has suffered discrimination historically comes into play. For example, women have suffered unequal treatment and therefore classification based on gender is one with a history of discrimination, but classification based on the result of a driver's test is not. Third, the court must consider whether there has been a lack of full protection through a political procedure such as legislation, and thus, whether there is a likelihood of continued use of a certain characteristic as the basis for discrimination. In other words, if the court has failed to give full protection to groups who are treated differently, it becomes difficult for these groups to be treated equally through legislation. For example, African Americans as a minority group find it difficult to gain equal treatment. Therefore, acts involving African Americans become more suspect.[17]

So, does classification based on gender have a higher degree of suspiciousness? In terms of their proportion in the population females are not a minority. Theoretically, they have the full ability to influence political procedures in seeking equal treatment. However, as some scholars point out, females may not be a minority in the population, but the majority of officials in Congress, governments, and courts are male. This means that females may still suffer unequal treatment in a political procedure.[18]

Based on these three elements, the US Supreme Court determines the type and degree of suspiciousness of classification and further clarifies applicable criteria of review. In practice, classification based on race and national origin is considered suspect and calls for applying the strict scrutiny test. Classification based on gender and whether one was born in or out of wedlock requires an intermediate scrutiny test. Classification based on age and wealth and sexual orientation is not suspect and only needs the rational basis test.

Determining whether fundamental rights are involved. When the Supreme Court selects the review criteria, aside from considering the types of classification, it also analyzes whether the classification involves fundamental rights. If it involves fundamental rights, the classification will receive the strict scrutiny test. The court's earliest use of the equal protection clause to protect fundamental rights was in *Skinner v. Oklahoma* (1942). The Oklahoma Habitual Criminal Sterilization Act required surgical sterilization for individuals who had been convicted three or more times for crimes involving "moral turpitude." The court held the right to procreate was a fundamental right and the strict scrutiny test should be applied. This was the first time the court used the term *strict scrutiny test*.[19] In *Zablocki v. Redhail* (1978), the court affirmed this doctrine in a case involving a Wisconsin law that prohibited individuals who had child-support obligations from getting married without a judicial determination that the individual's child-support obligations were being met and would continue to be met. The court held that the Wisconsin law interfered with the fundamental right of marriage so the strict scrutiny test had to be applied. In the end, the court declared that this law was unconstitutional because it did not meet the strict scrutiny standard.[20]

Which rights, then, are fundamental rights? From the point of view of the Supreme Court, fundamental rights are not restricted to those explicitly listed in the Constitution. Aside from rights, such as the right to vote, which are stipulated in the First to Eighth amendments,[21] through its interpretation of the Ninth and the Fifth amendments in cases that have set a precedent, the court has also confirmed that fundamental rights include the unlisted right of marriage,[22] the right to procreate,[23] the right to access the courts,[24] and the right to interstate travel.[25]

Review of purpose and method. After determining the standard of review, the court will use these criteria to review the propriety of the purpose and the connection between the purpose and method of classification. As for purpose, if the strict scrutiny test is conducted, the purpose of classification must be a compelling governmental purpose. The court usually reviews the wording of the law and its application in specific settings to determine whether the benefit it wants to achieve is compelling. Under such circumstances, it is difficult for the law to pass scrutiny; only a small number are deemed as conforming to the requirements. If it is a rational basis test, legitimate (as opposed to compelling) purpose can pass scrutiny. The court usually respects the government's selection and accepts the government's purpose, such as public safety, public health, and public morality. However, purposes prohibited by the Constitution will not be deemed legitimate—restrictions on freedom of religion[26] and freedom of speech, for example.[27] The intermediate scrutiny test that lies between the strict scrutiny test and the rational basis test demands that the purpose be important, if not compelling.

Additionally, the court reviews the connection between purpose and method that is to determine the relationship between the groups the classification intends to cover and the groups actually covered.[28] If the actual covered groups are fewer than the groups the purpose wants to cover, the classification fails to be inclusive. On the other hand, if the actual covered groups are more than those the purpose intends to cover, the classification is over-inclusive. The ideal condition is when the actual covered groups and the groups the purpose intends to cover are identical. In fact, classification often is under- or over-inclusive although this does not necessarily mean it cannot pass the scrutiny test. The court investigates under- and over-inclusiveness to confirm the degree of connection between method and purpose.

Different review criteria have different requirements for the degree of connection between method and purpose. The strict scrutiny test requires that the law or regulation is necessary for achieving a compelling governmental purpose. At such times, the government needs to prove that it not only can achieve this purpose, but that the method it uses to do so is also the least restrictive alternative. If there is no other feasible and less restrictive method to achieve the purpose, this method will be deemed the least restrictive alternative. If a less restrictive method is available, this method will not be deemed the least restrictive alternative for achieving the purpose. In applying the rational basis test, as long as the method helps to achieve the purpose, it may pass the test. In *McGowan v. Maryland* (1961), the court noted, "The court has held that the Fourteenth Amendment permits the State a wide scope of discretion in enacting laws which affect some groups of citizens differently from others. The constitutional safeguard is offended only if a classification rests on ground wholly irrelevant to the achievement of the State's objective. State legislatures are presumed to have acted within their constitutional power despite the fact that in practice their law results in some inequality."[29] In other words, the laws will be upheld unless the state's action is "clearly wrong, a display of arbitrary power, not an exercise of judgment."[30] The intermediate scrutiny test requires that there be substantial connection between the means and the end. In *Craig v. Boren* (1976), the Supreme Court noted under intermediate scrutiny that a law is upheld if it is substantially related to an important government purpose.[31]

Applying the Framework for Analysis in China

Equal protection review in the United States revolves around the selection of various criteria to be used in conducting the review. First there must be a classification. Then, based on the type of classification and whether it interferes with a fundamental right, the court determines the review criteria, that is, strict scrutiny, intermediate scrutiny, or the rational basis test. Finally, the justices use specific criteria to conduct the review of purpose and method, and then they make a decision.

The framework for analysis provides the judge with a path and method of review, so that the judge does not have to start from scratch every time he or she encounters a case. This is a great help to the judge under pressure from the number of lawsuits and time constraints for deciding them. At the same time, the framework for analysis is also a restriction for the judge, who has to select and apply suitable criteria. This does not mean, of course, that the judge is strictly limited to following precedents. Standards may have changed with changing social contexts. However, if the judge thinks that precedents are not suitable for this case, he or she must fully expound the reasons. For example, in the 1954 *Brown* case, by expounding the value of education for an individual's success, and finding that racial segregation was a detrimental influence on the physical and mental health of African American children, the US Supreme Court was able to show that the principle of "separate but equal" established by the 1896 *Plessy* case was not suitable and proclaimed that the segregation of schools was unconstitutional.[32]

While the framework for analysis allows flexibility to the judge, it also prevents the judge from being reckless. The judge is like a dancer dancing in shackles—dancing with the actual situation of a case but unable to deviate from the rules of the dance. As noted above, since the 2003 case about "height discrimination," in China, quite a few cases have concerned interference with equal rights. Nevertheless, the Supreme Court has not made any judicial interpretations and neither have related precedents been formed in judicial practice, let alone a systematic equal protection doctrine. Under such conditions, it is necessary to introduce a framework for analysis for equal protection review into China. When there is a framework for analysis, a judge will be clear as to what steps to include, what elements should be considered, and how to analyze specific cases for review. This not only helps to solve the problem of how to try cases when encountering them; it also helps to ensure that trials taking place at different times and in different places would still have uniformity. After all, the framework for analysis is a restriction on the judge, ensuring that the process of judgment will unfold following established procedure and steps, thus further guaranteeing that the law will be applied in a unified way. With regard to China, which has not yet realized the rule of law, and whose frequency of amendment to laws is quite high, stability of law has special significance.

How Should the Chinese Court Approach Application?

The framework for analysis supplies the approach for the judge and provides a structure for thinking about the judgment. However, a framework is not enough to arrive at the judgment of a case. The framework must be filled with specific content. Can we directly introduce the specific contents of the equal protection review doctrine of the United States into China?

As noted above, the US Supreme Court gradually formed the standards of equal protection review through precedents. The strict scrutiny test is applied whenever classification involving basic rights, race, and national origin is suspected. Classification based on gender, national origin, and whether one was born in wedlock is semi-suspect and the intermediate scrutiny test is applied. It is clear that classification based on race, gender, national origin, and those cases involving basic rights have a higher degree of suspicion. Minorities, females, immigrants, and individuals' basic rights should receive stronger protection.

Actually, the Chinese Constitution and laws embody a similar spirit. For example, Article 34 of the Constitution stipulates that all citizens of the People's Republic of China who have reached the age of 18 have the right to vote and stand for election, regardless of ethnic status, race, gender, occupation, family background, religious belief, education, property status, or length of residence; the article excepts persons whom the law has deprived of political rights. Article 48 says that women in the People's Republic of China enjoy equal rights with men in all spheres of life, in political, economic, cultural, social, and family life. Article Three of the Employment Promotion Law stipulates that workers enjoy equal rights to employment in jobs of their choosing. In seeking employment, workers shall not be subject to discrimination because of their ethnic background, race, gender, religious beliefs, and so on. Race, ethnic background, and gender are innate and immutable, and the classifications based on these characteristics are more suspect and should receive a strict scrutiny test. And religious belief is a fundamental right stipulated in the Chinese Constitution. In this respect, if a classification interferes with fundamental rights and the characteristics are clearly listed by law, it should receive the same strict scrutiny test.

The next question to be asked is: what are fundamental rights? The Supreme Court of the United States has clarified the fundamental rights that can be subjected to a strict scrutiny test; they include the right to vote, the right of marriage, the right to procreate, the right to access the courts, and the right to interstate travel. These rights not only include those explicitly listed in the Constitution, but also rights not listed but deduced from the interpretation of the Constitution. In addition to the right of private property in Article 13, Chapter 2 of the Chinese Constitution stipulates citizens' fundamental rights, including the right to vote, freedom of speech, the press, and assembly, of association, of procession, and of demonstration, freedom of religious belief, the freedom and privacy of correspondence, the right to criticize and make suggestions, the right of appeal, the right to accuse and report, the right to work, the right to receive an education, and the freedom to engage in scientific research. In this respect, the scope of fundamental rights differs in China and in the United States. The US Supreme Court deems the right to choose schools to be a fundamental right, but does not believe that the right to education is a fundamental one.[33] Thus, it is necessary to confirm whether a classification interferes with fundamental rights based on the stipulations in the Chinese Constitution, and to select suitable review criteria. The key issues are whether the right in question belongs within the scope of rights clearly listed in the Constitution (such as the right to access the courts), whether it is a fundamental right, and whether the classification interfering with this right should receive the strict scrutiny test—in other words, whether the Chinese court can deduce new fundamental rights through interpretation of the Constitution and then conduct a strict scrutiny test. The answer to this question is related to the legal traditions and to the authority for interpretation of the Constitution in different countries.

The United States is a country with a common law legal system. The judicial precedents created by judges are important components of its legal system. And the Constitution of the United States is mainly interpreted by the court. If it involves lawsuits, the US Supreme Court has the last word. Based on this power, the US court can deduce new basic rights through its interpretation of the Constitution.

China is a country with a continental legal system. The power of making law is exercised by the legislative organ that represents the people; the duty of the judge is to apply the law to disputes and judge cases based on the law. Even though the judge is not a mere "mouthpiece of the law," still the judge's duty is to apply laws and not to create laws. Once the judgment goes beyond the law, its legitimacy will be suspect. Moreover, according to the Constitution, it is the National People's Congress and its Standing Committee that interpret the Constitution and supervise its implementation. Even though this does not prevent the court from interpreting the Constitution during the process of trial, the court does not deem interpreting the Constitution to be its duty. In fact, the court has never interpreted the Constitution. The Supreme People's Court has said, officially, that it is not suitable to cite the Constitution as the basis for sentencing crimes. What is even more interesting is that on June 28, 2001, the Supreme People's Court passed "an official response concerning whether persons violating the fundamental right to education by violation of the right to name should bear civil liabilities" (*Judicial Interpretation* [2001] No. 25). This interpretation[34] was termed China's *Marbury v. Madison* and was believed to be the pioneer for constitutional review and triggered enthusiastic discussions in academic circles.[35] Following this official response, however, the Supreme People's Court did not interpret any articles of the Constitution and did not determine whether any laws, rules, and regulations were unconstitutional. Furthermore, on December 8, 2008, the Supreme People's Court stopped the application of *Judicial Interpretation* (2001) No. 25. It is not feasible for the Chinese courts to interpret the Constitution, and deduce "unlisted fundamental rights." Just conducting strict scrutiny tests for classifications interfering with the listed rights is more realistic.

Classifications based on the listed characteristics or interfering with fundamental rights should receive strict scrutiny tests. Then, is it to be the strict test or the intermediate test? Should the affirmative action based on these characteristics be subjected to a strict scrutiny test? Can the specific methods of the US court be used by the Chinese court? To answer these questions, we need to first clarify the basis for the review.

First, the selection of criteria is related to specific social context. As noted above, the US Supreme Court determines the standard in accordance with the level of discrimination. The court usually considers three aspects: whether the characteristics for classification are innate, whether the groups being treated differently have been discriminated against historically, and whether these groups can seek equal treatment through political process by legislation and other political procedures. If the specific groups were discriminated against and if it is difficult to obtain equal treatment through changing the characteristics that the classification was based on or through political channels, this type of classification will receive a strict scrutiny test. This method considers the influence on a specific group in a comprehensive manner and determines the criteria for review based on the decision. This is not to say, however, that when the classification fits the three characteristics listed above, it is a suspect classification, and when it fits two, it is a semi-suspect classification.

For example, as noted above, gender is innate and immutable and females have suffered discrimination historically. Even though the proportion of females is not low in the total population, the proportion of female senators and members of Congress is not high; therefore it is difficult for women to seek equal treatment through the political process. A gender-based classification completely fits the three characteristics, but the court does not view it as a suspect classification; it is classified as semi-suspect, which calls for the intermediate scrutiny test. Furthermore, the review criterion applied to a gender-based classification has had a process of change. Before the 1970s, the courts applied the rational basis test to gender-based classifications. In *Bradwell v. Illinois* (1873),[36] *Muller v. Oregon* (1908),[37] *Hoyt v. Florida* (1961),[38] and even *Reed v. Reed* (1971)[39] if a gender-based classification was rational and related to a legitimate state purpose, it was deemed constitutional. However, in *Frontiero v. Richardson* (1973)[40] there arose differences among the Supreme Court justices as to which standard of review to apply to a gender-based classification: four judges believed precedents should be overthrown and the strict scrutiny test applied, but the rest still insisted on applying the rational basis test. In *Craig v. Boren* (1976),[41] after looking back at the principles of the *Reed* and *Frontiero* cases, the court pointed out that "previous cases establish that classification by gender must serve important governmental objectives and must be substantially related to achievement of those interests." Thus, it established the standard of intermediate scrutiny for gender-based classification. From then on, courts have followed this principle. In recent years there has appeared the tendency to practice even more strict review of the classification. The majority opinion in *United States v. Virginia* (1996), written by Justice Ruth Bader Ginsburg, pointed out that gender-based classification should be exceedingly persuasive.[42]

The changes of gender-based classification review criteria are related to the strength of the law protecting women's rights and interests and the whole society's identification with equality for women and the rise of the women's movement. Neither the Declaration of Independence, which declares that "everyone is born equal," nor the US Constitution, whose aim is to safeguard individual rights, mentions women's rights. Even after the 14th Amendment was passed in 1868, this clause was not believed to provide strong legal protection for females. It is rather interesting that when the "Statue of Liberty illuminating the world" was unveiled on October 28, 1886, females could not participate in the unveiling ceremony. Some progressive females organized themselves and rented a boat to Bedloe's Island to protest. Thus arose the early women's rights movement demanding equality for women and striving for political rights. Finally in 1920, Congress passed the 19th Amendment, which prohibited depriving US citizens of the right to vote based on gender. However, the court only interpreted this amendment as protecting women's right to vote and rarely considered it as applying to other forms of equality.[43]

It was not until the 1960s, when the United States faced the problems of serious racial antagonism, the growing gap between the rich and the poor, and involvement in the Vietnam War that people became strongly dissatisfied with society, which gave rise to the Civil Rights Movement, the anti-war movement, youth rebellion, and the women's rights movement. All these phenomena not only helped women more fully understand themselves, but also changed society's stereotype of them, and the idea of equality for women became widely accepted. With this background, the Supreme Court raised the strength of the review and gave women stronger legal protection.

We can see from this that there is no mathematical formula to determine classification types and their review criteria. The selection of criteria is actually related to the specific context of a society. China and the United States face many different social problems and issues of treatment of specific groups. Applying the US criteria in China would not be feasible. Second, equal protection review involves value judgments. The court needs to judge whether it should require treating all people equally or to give some people different treatment to make up for past discrimination. In order to realize equality, does it only need to withdraw the classifications that discriminate against specific groups or to take specific measures to reduce the difference between groups? In other words, should equality be formal or should it be substantive? Should the government actively promote substantive equality?[44] Those are value judgments. The answers are not objective and inevitable. On the contrary, they are related to legal traditions and social ideas. The selection in different countries may be different, and the selection at different times may also be different.

In fact, the selection by the US Supreme Court is not unchanging. The review of affirmative action aimed at giving minorities more opportunities is direct evidence. Affirmative action refers to state action that gives certain opportunities or benefits to specific groups.[45] The purpose is to balance the inferior positions of these groups to assist them in realizing personal freedom and self-development so as to reach substantive equality. The difference between this and the general differential treatment is that the latter gives a specific group unfavorable treatment, while the former provides special benefits so as to change the unfavorable condition of a group. Therefore, the US Chief Justice calls affirmative action a "benign classification."[46] Even though it is benign, affirmative action means distinct treatment to different groups, so the court has to conduct a constitutional review. The Supreme Court sometimes adopts the intermediate scrutiny test to support affirmative action.[47] Sometimes justices who tend to favor equality for people of color will conduct a strict scrutiny test of affirmative action unless the action is necessary to meet a compelling governmental interest. Otherwise, the action will be struck down. In *Richmond City v. J. A. Croson Co.* (1989),[48] the court pointed out that race-based affirmative action policies, at least at the state and local level, should be subjected to strict scrutiny analysis and that such programs must be narrowly tailored to address identifiable forms of past discrimination; it struck down Richmond's set-aside program for public contracts. From then on, the court has applied the strict scrutiny test to race-based affirmative action.

Some scholars have challenged the court's "color-blind" application of the strict scrutiny test to affirmative action. Sunstein thought that equal protection should analyze the relationship between different groups and change actual unequal conditions.[49] In reality, even though the court applies the strict scrutiny test, it does not overthrow all affirmative action. In *Grutter v. Bollinger* (2003), the court supported the affirmative action policies of the University of Michigan Law School. Some scholars even believed that the Supreme Court did not apply the strict scrutiny test during this case, but actually applied the intermediate scrutiny test. To establish the principle of applying an intermediate scrutiny test to affirmative action measures for universities is beneficial but, in fact, the court did not do it this way.[50]

The Supreme Court applies the strict scrutiny test to race-based classifications, no matter whether the classification is affirmative action. This means the state should treat every race and every person in the same way, unless the governmental interest is very important and the classification is necessary. That is to say, equality in form is the principle. This concept can be traced back to the "American dream"—that is, people must achieve success through their own hard work, rather than relying on specific family background, social position, and other people's help. And the American dream is embodied in the Constitution.

The Chinese Constitution, however, while stipulating formal equality, emphasizes at the same time that the country should actively adopt measures to promote substantive equality. For example, the second clause of Article Four stipulates that the state assists areas inhabited by minority nationalities in accelerating their economic and cultural development according to the characteristics and needs of the various minority nationalities. The second clause of the 48th Article says that the state protects the rights and interests of women, applies the principle of equal pay for equal work to men and women alike, and trains and selects cadres from among women. This is not only related to the objectives of a socialist constitution, but it coincides with traditional Chinese ideas. The Chinese Constitution continues to be influenced by the Soviet Constitution. The aim of the Soviet Socialist revolution was to overthrow the capitalist system and to safeguard the workers' right to have a human life.[51] The Soviet Constitution formulated after the successful revolution emphasizes substantive equality. The Chinese Constitution inherited this tradition and established related articles and clauses in the Constitution. Furthermore, in China, there is a very long history of the concept of benevolent policies of caring for the people and equality for the poor and rich. The masses not only seek substantive equality, they trust and rely on the state to achieve this equality. This is obviously different from the state of affairs in the United States, which upholds formal equality and the concept of limited government. Considering this, perhaps it is more reasonable, in China, to conduct a less strict review of affirmative action.

Third, the standard of review is related to the position of the court, which is limited to the court's jurisdiction. When the court applies the strict scrutiny test, that is judicial activism. When it conducts its review, the court would not avoid confrontation with political organs and adopts the position that if necessary, it will not hesitate to declare that a law or an action is unconstitutional.[52] On the contrary, if it conducts a lesser review, the court will presume that the classification is constitutional, unless the purpose of the classification violates the prohibited stipulations in the Constitution, or the means are obviously not related to the purpose. That is judicial passivism. Whether the court is active or passive it is restricted by the specific political system and the court's jurisdiction. If taking an active position, the court will no longer presume that the decisions made by the legislative or administrative branches are constitutional, but will strictly examine the decisions. While the Constitution needs to be interpreted, the court may force its own understanding on other branches in the name of the Constitution and will be under suspicion of interfering with other branches. The more positivist the position of the court, the greater the power of reviews, and the more deeply the court becomes involved in the political battle. Whether the court can exercise such strong power is determined by the limitations on its jurisdiction.

In the United States, separation of powers and checks and balances are fundamental principles of the political system. The court has the authority to review the constitutionality of the actions of Congress or the president. In a judgment, the court can even express its opinion as to how to adopt affirmative action to change past discrimination. In *Swann v. Charlotte-Mecklenburg Board of Education* (1971), the Supreme Court affirmed this power. The court upheld court-ordered bussing as a method of achieving school desegregation.[53]

The political system and the jurisdiction of the court in China are different. First, there is a distinction between the functions of the National People's Congress and the Supreme People's Court: the National People's Congress is responsible for legislation and the court exercises the power of trial. The National People's Congress has the highest power in the country. The 57th Article of the Constitution stipulates that. Furthermore, according to the 62nd and 63rd articles of the Constitution, the National People's Congress has the power to elect the president of the Supreme People's Court and to recall or remove the president of the Supreme People's Court from office. The 128th Article also stipulates that the Supreme People's Court is responsible to the National People's Congress and its Standing Committee. Local people's courts at different levels are responsible to the organs of state power, which created them. In this respect, China is more similar to Great Britain where Parliament is supreme.

Second, for a long time, in China the court was viewed as a part of the government, and even after judicial reform, the independence of the court is still in the process of being established. When the New China was set up, the court was established. But at that time, the court was a tool of the rulers. This view was criticized after the reform and opening up of the country. The reform was deemed not only to safeguard the interests of the state, but also to safeguard the people's rights.[54] However, the funding of the courts depends on the governments. In this respect, the court is a rather weak branch. It is owing to this that, in recent years, academics have enthusiastically discussed how to establish an independent judicial fiscal system and this has also become the focus of judicial reform.

Third, China is a country with a continental legal system. In this tradition, the legislative organ is responsible for drafting the law and the function of the court is to apply the law.

Compared to the American court, the jurisdiction of the Chinese court is smaller and it is a weaker branch among all of the state organs. Owing to this, the Chinese court may not adopt a positive position.

Finally, the triple criteria for review are only a simplification of the different standards of review; each criterion can still be further divided. Thus, they form a complex system.[55] The strict scrutiny test is strict in theory, and fatal in fact,[56] and the rational basis test is minimal scrutiny in theory and virtually nonexistent in fact.[57] These are only rough descriptions of how the system operates. In reality, what the US Supreme Court applies is a spectrum of standards of review. Sometimes the rational basis criterion can also have "bite". The intermediate scrutiny test is basically not very different from the rational basis test in some cases, but similar to the strict scrutiny test in others.

Some scholars believe the US Supreme Court changes the rules of review based on reasons and methods for race-based classification. In fact, there are at least three different versions of a strict scrutiny test that were applied in cases involving racial redistricting, affirmative action, and racial profiling. However, the court still insists that what it applies is a standard called the strict scrutiny test. The reason could be that justices are not elected. If the court forms different standards to suit different policy areas, the court becomes a policymaker.[58] After making a systematic empirical study of strict scrutiny applied by Supreme Courts between 1990 and 2003, Winkler said that strict scrutiny is far from the inevitably deadly test imagined by the Gunther myth and more closely resembles the context-sensitive tool described by O'Connor. Courts routinely uphold laws when applying strict scrutiny, and they do so in every major area of law in which they use the test.[59] He also mentioned a contextual strict scrutiny test, but did not explain how to apply it.[60]

As to how to apply a contextual strict scrutiny test, scholars believe four aspects should be considered. First, take racial group history and current racial conditions into account. Second, distinguish classifications designed to promote inclusion from those designed to exclude particular groups, especially groups historically excluded from the opportunities and benefits of mainstream American life by law and social practice. Third, check whether initiatives designed to address group-based forms of exclusion and inequality may actually be motivated by prejudice or harmful stereotypes. Finally, check to see that the government considered a range of realistic alternatives and, if it did so, then accord a measure of judicial respect to the government's selected means for addressing long-standing group disadvantages.[61] This method considers the condition of specific groups in a comprehensive manner and strives to include specific groups who have suffered discrimination. This is helpful in correcting discrimination and remedying the harmful influence of discrimination. However, the experiences of specific groups may not be the same in different countries. Therefore, the review needs to consider specific situations. This method limits the scope of review to procedures carried out by the state and keeps the court from expressing opinions on actual disputes and becoming involved in arguments related to public policy. This may be a suitable choice for the Chinese court, which is still a branch with weak powers. If the court only reviews the procedure, the strict review may in fact change into a rational basis review. Therefore, the court should consider whether the governmental purpose is compelling, and the act is narrowly tailored to meet a compelling governmental interest. The court needs to evaluate whether the governmental interest or the specific group's interest is more important. And the evaluation of interest is not universal.

In summary, the determination of review criteria involves different values and different viewpoints. This is not only related to the specific social context created by the politics, economy, and culture of each country, but it is restricted by each country's system and by the jurisdiction and function of the court established by the system. Because of this, we can introduce the framework of equal protection review of the United States to China, but cannot apply all of the methods to Chinese judicial practice. Of course, this does not mean that we cannot introduce certain specific American doctrines into China. However, we need to establish a system based on our own situation, and then apply certain criteria to individual cases.

The next question is what method we should adopt to design China's equal protection doctrine. Equal protection review is contextualized, and the design of this doctrine is still at a preliminary stage in China. The feasibility of specific methods still has to be tested in practice. Setting up a systematic standard immediately may not be feasible. So, it may be better to proceed by analyzing cases, clarifying the criteria and method to be applied to each one, and then extracting the common principles therein to gradually establish an equal protection doctrine.

Endnotes

[1] For instance, Berman believes that the globalization of law is "the Americanization of law." See "From the Globalization of Law to Law under Globalization," translated by Liu Hui, in *Transplantation of Law and Legal Culture*, edited by D. Nelken and J. Feaster, translated by Gao Hongjun, et al. (Qinghua University Press, 2006), 157. Also see Martin Shapiro, "The Globalization of Law," *Global Legal Studies Journal* vol.1 (1993): 61.

[2] He Yonghong, "Thoughts on the Constitutionality of China's First Case in Hepatitis B Discrimination," *Zhongnan University Reports* (Social Sciences edition) vol. 5 (2006).

[3] Wang Hanbin, "On 'People's Republic of China Administrative Procedural Law' (draft)," in *The Complete Report by the People's Supreme Court (1985—1994)* (People's Court Publisher, 1995), 42.

[4] See "Notice of the Supreme People's Court on the Publishing and Distributing of 'On the Summary of the Forum on the Problem of Applying Legal Standards in Administrative Case Trials'" (Law, 2004, No. 96).

[5] See "Notice of the Publication and Distribution of the Second Group of Guiding Precedent Cases by the Supreme People's Court" (Law, 2012, No. 172).

[6] Daniel E. Hall and John P. Feldmeier, *Constitutional Law: Governmental Powers and Individual Freedoms*, 2nd ed. (New Jersey: Prentice Hall, 2012), 453.

[7] Joseph Tussman and Jacobus Tenbroke, "Equal Protection of Laws," *California Law Review* 37 (1949): 341.

[8] *Sweatt v. Painter*, 339 U.S. 629 (1950).

[9] Erwin Chemerinsky, *Constitutional Law: Principles and Policies*, 3rd ed. (New York: Aspen Publisher, 2006), 670.

[10] *Washington v. Davis*, 426 U.S. 229 (1976).

[11] *Personnel Administrator of Massachusetts v. Feeney*, 442 U.S. 256 (1979); *Mobile v. Bolden*, 446 U.S. 55 (1980); *Rogers v. Lodge*, 458 U.S. 613 (1982); *McCleskey v. Kemp*, 481 U.S. 279 (1987).

[12] Erwin Chemerinsky, *Constitutional Law: Principles and Policies*, 676.

[13] *Shelley v. Kraemer*, 334 U.S. 1 (1948).

[14] *Jones v. Alfred H. Mayer Co.*, 392 U.S. 409 (1968).

[15] Erwin Chemerinsky, *Constitutional Law: Principles and Policies*, 672.

[16] See *Kahn v. Shevin*, 416 U.S. 351, 356 (1974); *Fullilover v. Klutznick*, 448 U.S. 448, 496 (1980).

[17] *Graham v. Richardson*, 403 U.S. 365, 367 (1971).

[18] Daniel Hall and John Feldmeier, *Constitutional Law: Governmental Powers and Individual Freedoms*, 450.

[19] *Skinner v. Oklahoma*, 316 U.S. 535 (1942).

[20] *Zablocki v. Redhail*, 434 U.S. 374 (1978).

[21] *Reynolds v. Sims*, 377 U.S. 533 (1964); *Harper v. Board of Education*, 383 U.S. 663 (1966); *Bush v. Gore*, 531 U.S. 98 (2000).

[22] *Zablocki v. Redhail*, 434 U.S. 374 (1978).

[23] *Skinner v. Oklahoma*, 316 U.S. 535 (1942).

[24] *Griffin v. Illinois*, 351 U.S. 12 (1956); *Douglas v. California*, 372 U.S. 353 (1963); *Boddie v. Connecticut*, 401 U.S. 371 (1971).

[25] *Shapiro v. Thompson*, 394 U.S. 618 (1969).

[26] *Romer v. Evans*, 517 U.S. 620 (1996).

[27] *U.S. Dept. of Agriculture. v. Moreno*, 413 U.S. 528, 534 (1973).

[28] Joseph Tussman and Jacobus Tenbroke, "The Equal Protection of Laws," 348-353.

[29] *McGowan v. Maryland*, 366 U.S. 420, 425-426 (1961).

[30] *Mathews v. DeCastro*, 429 U.S. 181, 185 (1976).

[31] *Craig v. Boren*, 429 U.S.190 (1976).

[32] *Brown v. Board of Education of Topeka, Kansas*, 347 U.S. 483 (1954).

[33] *San Antonio Independent School District v. Rodriguez*, 411 U.S. 1 (1973).

[34] On the same day this reply was issued, President Huang Yousong of the first court of the Supreme People's Court published an article "Judicial Implementation of the Constitution and Its Meaning—from today's reply by the Supreme People's Court" in *People's Court* in which he cited the verdict of Chief Justice John Marshall in *Marbury v. Madison*, highly praised this reply, and described it as a forerunner of "judicial implementation of the constitution."

[35] See Miguel Schor, "Forward: Symposium on Constitutional Review in China," *Suffolk University Law Review* 43 (2010): 589; Zhiwei Tong, "A Comment on the Rise and Fall of the Supreme People's Court's Reply to Qi Yuling's Case," *Suffolk University Law Review* 43 (2010): 669; Larry C. Backer, "A Constitutional Court for China within the Chinese Communist Party?: Scientific Development and a Reconsideration of the Institutional Role of the CCP," *Suffolk University Law Review* 43 (2010): 593.

[36] *Bradwell v. Illinois*, 83 U.S. 130 (1873).

[37] *Muller v. Oregon*, 208 U.S. 412 (1908).

[38] *Hoyt v. Florida*, 368 U.S. 57 (1961).

[39] *Reed v. Reed*, 404 U.S. 71 (1971).

[40] *Frontiero v. Richardson*, 411 U.S. 677 (1973).

[41] *Craig v. Boren*, 429 U.S. 190 (1976).

[42] *United States v. Virginia*, 518 U.S. 515 (1996).

[43] Daniel Hall and John Feldmeier, *Constitutional Law: Governmental Powers and Individual Freedoms*, 467-470.

[44] Julie A. Nice, "Symposium: Discrimination and Inequality Emerging Issues Equal Protection's Antinomies and the Promise of a Co-constitutive Approach," *Cornell Law Review* 85 (2000): 1392.

[45] *Affirmative action* is also translated as "positive action," "correction action," or "favorable measures." At first it meant the measures the American government practiced in privileging minority races and women. Later it extended to the favorable practices towards all groups that had suffered differential treatment.

[46] *Regents of the University of California v. Bakke*, 438 U.S. 265 (1978).

[47] During the 1980 *Fullilove v. Kluznick* case, the court applied the intermediate scrutiny test in supporting the use of 10 percent of the foundation's funds for minority business. In *Metro Broadcasting Inc. v. Federal Communications Commission* (1990), the court also applied the intermediate scrutiny test and supported constitutionality of the affirmative action by Congress. See *Fullilove v. Klutznick*, 448 U.S. 448 (1980); *Metro Broadcasting, Inc. v. Federal Communications Commission*, 497 U.S. 547 (1990).

[48] *City of Richmond v. J.A. Croson Co.*, 488 U.S. 469 (1989).

[49] See Cass R. Sunstein, *Radicals in Robes: Why Extremist Right-Wing Courts Are Wrong for America* (New York: Basic Books, 2005), 132-133.

[50] Libby Huskey, "Constitutional Law—Affirmative Action in Higher Education—Strict in Theory, Intermediate in Fact? *Grutter v. Bollinger*, 123 S. Ct. 2325 (2003)," *Wyoming Law Review* 4 (2004): 439.

[51] Sugihara Yasuo: *History of Constitutions—New Theory of Comparative Study of Constitutions*, translated by Lü Xu and Qu Tao (Social Sciences Document Publisher, 2000), 146.

[52] Abe Teraya, et al., eds. *Constitutions (1)*, translated by Zhou Zongxian (Chinese Political and Law University Publisher, 2006), 402.

[53] *Swann v. Charlotte-Mecklenburg Board of Education*, 402 U.S.28, 30-31 (1974).

[54] Guo Daohui, "Diversity and Socialization of Power," *Law Studies* No.1 (2001); Qi Duojun, "On Power," *Law Studies* No.1 (2001).

[55] Kelso divides equal protection review into nine kinds. See R. Randall Kelso, "Standard of Review under the Equal Protection Clause and Related Constitutional Doctrines Protecting

Individual Rights: The "'Base Plus Six'" Model and Modern Supreme Court Practice," *University of Pennsylvania Journal of Constitutional Law* 4 (2002): 225.

[56] Gerald Gunther, "The Supreme Court, 1971 Term—Foreword: In Search of Evolving Doctrine on a Changing Court: A Model for a Newer Equal Protection," *Harvard Law Review* 86 (1972): 1, 8.

[57] Gerald Gunther and Kathleen M. Sullivan, *Constitutional Law*, 13th ed. (Westbury, NY: Foundation Press, 1997), 602.

[58] Evan Gerstmann and Christopher Shortell, "The Many Faces of Strict Scrutiny: How the Supreme Court Changes the Rules in Race Cases," *University of Pittsburgh Law Review* 72 (2001): 1.

[59] *Grutter v. Bollinger*, 539 U.S. 306 (2003).

[60] Adam Winkler, "Fatal in Theory and Strict in Fact: An Empirical Analysis of Strict Scrutiny in the Federal Courts," *Vanderbilt Law Review* 59 (2006): 793.

[61] Eric K. Yamamoto, Carly Minner, and Karen Winter, "Contextual Strict Scrutiny," *Harvard Law Journal* 49 (2006): 241.

Jing Zhou is an associate professor at the Institute of American Studies, Chinese Academy of Social Sciences (IAS, CASS). A specialist in comparative law, she is the author of A Critical Legal Ideal: Reconstruction of Judicial Foundation and Method, *published in 2010. Before joining IAS, she was a postdoctoral researcher at the Institute of Sociology, CASS where she received the Outstanding Prize awarded by the China Postdoctoral Science Foundation in 2009.*

6

Putting Our Minds Together for a Better Future

by
Harley Eagle

"Let us put our minds together and see what life we can make for our children."

—Tatanka Iyotake-Sitting Bull
Hunkpapa Lakota Healer and Leader

In late December of 2012, Jim Yellowhawk, his son Gabe, and I travelled back to *the land of the long white cloud*, Aotearoa (New Zealand), to reconnect with friends and colleagues we had met on previous trips. The trip was taken under the auspices of the first ever Ruth Yellowhawk Fellowship on Native American Forums, which was established by the Kettering Foundation in Ruth's memory.* The fellowship supports grass-

---

* The Ruth Yellowhawk Fellowship was established in 2010 after her untimely death. The goal of the fellowship is to recognize Ruth's tireless work sharing indigenous people's deliberative traditions and the role of deliberation in modern tribal decision making. Her work took her to New Zealand where she collaborated with Harley Eagle and her husband Jim in reclaiming cross-cultural tribal understandings of deliberation. The first fellowship completed the work Ruth, Jim and the author had begun. It also offered Jim, an accomplished artist, the opportunity to use his art to further the tribal connections he made while completing the research. This excerpt from a longer report is an account of Jim's use of art as a tribute to tribal culture that is often misunderstood.

roots researchers doing experiential and participatory work in communities in which they are already active, with a focus on the stories and experiences of either historical or contemporary decision making within American Indian indigenous culture.

This report does not illustrate the mechanics and science of decision making in the communities we write about. It does not use a scientific or Western academic approach that would entail studying each detail to learn its function and purpose. It attempts, rather, to articulate the relationships and spaces between the individuals involved.

At the time of this trip, Jim, a gifted and award-winning Native American artist, began a profound artistic process aimed at bringing together his Lakota heritage and culture with those of the indigenous people of Aotearoa and other indigenous Pacific Islanders. Its expression would be an art piece inspired by the experience the Yellowhawk family had during an earlier visit to the Maori community of Ohinemutu, Rotorua.

Art and the expression of his culture through dance and music is Jim's way of connecting with the people, the land, and the issues that communities face. In Aotearoa and back on his home territory in South Dakota some of these issues focus on how gangs affect youth, families, and communities. Sometimes the issues are about treaty violations or the legacy of the colonization of indigenous people. Fatherhood is also an important issue to Jim, who spent several days attending a conference in 2010 looking at the issue of what it means through indigenous eyes to be a father. He is concerned too about the effects of gambling addiction on communities. All of these problems are found in Aotearoa and in Native American communities in South Dakota as well as Canada. Yet another issue central to Jim's journey in life, and a part of his desire to come back to Aotearoa, is the honoring of indigenous World War II veterans. This leads to the story of what Jim saw at the Maori Marae in Rotorua in 2010 that would lead to a way of honoring both Jim's grandfather, a WWII veteran, and a Maori hero of the same war.

A *Marae* is the communal structure of the Maori people, considered sacred and special where ceremonies, important discussions, decision making, and other significant community events take place. It is a place that defines the identity of a particular tribe of the Maori nation so each place is full of unique carvings and other special items sacred and important to that specific area and the families who live there. During one such gathering at a

Marae in the Maori village of Ohinemutu in Rotorua, which is several hours northeast of Wellington, Jim could see the top of an old WWII army helmet that was situated on top of a five-foot-high Maori carving. His curiosity was piqued and, upon asking some of the local folks, he learned about the carving by local Maori artist Rakei Kingi that was dedicated and placed in the Marae in 2007. The carving honors Maori WWII hero Haane Te Rauawa Manahi.

Jim's grandfather, Bert Yellowhawk, was also a distinguished American veteran of the Second World War. It had long been Jim's hope to find a way to honor him. Hearing about Manahi's exceptional story sparked an idea in his mind: he would create an artwork that honored both men.

Haane Te Rauawa Manahi (1913-1986) is a significant and much loved person in the minds and hearts of the Maori people. He served in Greece, Crete, and North Africa during WWII. In particular he showed outstanding bravery under fire at a battle in Takrouna, Tunisia, leading his men to capture a vital enemy stronghold held by more than 300 Italian and German troops. Four generals recommended Manahi for Britain's highest war medal, a Victoria Cross (VC), but it was never awarded to him. The award was downgraded to a Distinguished Conduct Medal (DCM). Some say this was due to racist attitudes, which ensured that no (or at least not many) "colonials" would receive the VC. Others claim that there was a moratorium order issued on the awarding of VCs and Manahi was a victim of circumstance.

Manahi's son, Geoffrey, says that he asked his father about the Victoria Cross (Manahi 1998). His father's response: "Oh, who cares about the VC, forget it. There were many men in the 28th Maori Battalion who could easily have won that *Pākehā* ("white people") medal. Many of them died in the fire of battle." Manahi was extremely humble, according to his son. "The most important thing to him was his family, fishing, his wife—those were the important things in life to my father. The VC was not a major issue at all."

It was this humility, among other values, that Jim wanted to honor in both Manahi and in his grandfather Bert. Here, he speaks of his work:

> This artwork is in honor of my grandfather Bert Yellowhawk and Haane Manahi two amazing warriors—and all the men and women that have served their country. My name is Jim Yellowhawk. I am

Lakota and Iroquois from the Black Hills of South Dakota, US. I am a full-time Lakota artist and traditional Lakota dancer. This work started here in New Zealand (2010) and continued over the next two years. When I was in Rotorua I went to a conference here and learned about Haane Manahi and also the Te Papaiouru Marae, Ohinemutu where he was laid to rest. I was touched by his story and thought of my grandfather Bert Yellowhawk and his own time serving the US Army. Both men were a year apart in age and served during the same time. My grandfather was a Lakota from the Cheyenne River Reservation in South Dakota, US. I thought this would be a good painting showing two different cultures. Two different men, but with the same value systems and very much the same in almost everything. To honor them, I did this work when I went back to the United States in 2010.

This work is titled "Blood Warrior" and is done on ledger paper, which I found in New Zealand and which serves as the background. This Native American art form is called Ledger Art. I also used a WWII New Zealand military helmet to show the time period. The text that appears in the piece was composed by my wife Ruth Yellowhawk whose Lakota name was "Taho Kahwoka Win," Woman Whose Voice Is in the Air.

Returning to Aotearoa this year, I brought "Blood Warrior" to its new home and to where the idea, or vision, first came to me. I wanted to honor my wife Ruth Yellowhawk, Haane Manahi, and Bert Yellowhawk.

This was a healing journey for me and my son Gabe Yellowhawk. To present to Rau Manahi, Haane Manahi's son, was a high honor for me. I feel I have gone full circle with this piece. Mitakuye Oyasin, "We are all related." (Yellowhawk, personal communication, April 25, 2013).

Jim also talked about how important it was to him that his art piece express the humanity of these two men even in the context of bloody battles and war. He wanted to capture who these men were as human beings with deep values based on their indigenous cultures. Jim was able to collect a story via a response to an Internet post asking whether there was anyone who may have heard of Bert Yellowhawk while he served in the US army in Germany during World War II. This account arrived shortly before he presented the art piece to the son of Haane Manahi on the Marae in Rotorua on April 17, 2013. The story, as told by a grandson of a German army veteran, reflects the humanity of Jim's grandfather Bert Yellowhawk:

> My grandmother's brother, Rudolf Hanel (he will now be referred to as grandpa as this was our family tradition, to call our grandparent's brothers and sisters our grandparents too) served in the Wehrmacht, like everybody had to. In the winter of 1944-1945 he was stationed near the German border in a large forest. The US army had broken through the lines in the north and south of the area where my grandpa was; then they found out that they had the enemy in the back of their units. They tried to get back to their unit but their platoon leader panicked as he was new to this role and they got deeper into American-held territory.
>
> They had been short of ammo and had no food but later they ambushed some American vehicles and captured weapons, ammo, and food. Later in the day they had a big fight with strong American forces and my grandpa and one of his comrades had been separated from the rest of their platoon. It was getting dark and the temperature was dropping fast. You could not tell friend from foe in the large forest.
>
> Over the course of the day the German soldiers attacked and tried to recapture the lost ground. On both sides there had been many separated units because on that day there had been no common frontline. Night came and my grandpa and his comrade had to take shelter from the snow and cold in a half-burned-down cabin.
>
> It was dark when they heard voices outside the cabin but it was in a language they had never heard before. Then two men covered in wool blankets came into the cabin. Everybody began yelling, "Hands up, don't shoot, and so on." Then the four men lowered

their guns and they decided that there had been enough bloodshed for one day, grandpa told me. Those two soldiers were Native Americans. They started a fire and began to share their food. My grandpa had some tea and they shared a peaceful night.

My grandpa spoke a little bit of English so he could speak a little to the other soldiers. One man's name was Bert and my grandpa told him that was a common German name, and the man said his full name was Bertram, which also is a common, old German name. This man's family name was Yellow ... and then some predator bird like buzzard or hawk. Later my grandpa was sure it was hawk, Bert Yellowhawk. The name of the other man my grandpa could not remember. My grandpa said Bert had a beautiful face, just like some German boy would think an Indian would look like but only with short hair. Bert was a friendly, quiet man. It was like there was no war going on for that night.

My grandpa's brother had studied American history before the war and had told his brothers often about the genocide that had happened to the Indians in America. So my grandpa wanted to know how they could fight in the same army that put them on reservations. However his English was not good enough to ask the question but into his old age he always wondered.

The next morning they shared some cigarettes and food and then said goodbye. My grandpa and his comrade made it back to their unit and six weeks later he was taken prisoner of war by the Americans.

About a year after the war my grandpa thought he saw that same soldier, Bert Yellowhawk, in a town in Bavaria, still wearing his US military uniform. My grandpa was on a bus at the time and he saw the soldier on the street. He went back to look after he got off at the next stop but by that time the soldier was long gone. My grandpa always maintained he was sure it was the same man that he shared a brief break from the war all those years ago (Personal communication with J. Yellowhawk, January 2013).

The process of Jim gifting his art to the family of Haane Manahi is in keeping with indigenous protocols. It should be noted that these protocols are in some ways rigid but only in the sense that there must be some sort of ceremony attached to this type of occasion. The dynamics of how the ceremony falls into place tend to be much more natural, and based more on who is available and feels responsible for attending to the matter. There were several Maori people of the Te Papaiouru Marae who remained friends with the Yellowhawk family, in particular the Mitchell family who took this matter into their hands and worked to organize the ceremony, made sure that the appropriate people were notified, and looked after us while we were there. They treated us as special guests.

In fact, it felt to the three Native North Americans that they were treated as special guests and relatives wherever they visited in the Rotorua area. Rotorua is a special place known for its high number of Maori people still living there as well as the natural beauty of the area. It is a major tourist destination also known for the geothermal activity that accounts for the area's spectacular geysers, hot mud pools, and natural hot springs. It is also a place where you can find Maori people still steeped in their culture and committed to restoring cultural practices. As we were taken to visit several of the sites in the area, we often fell into discussions comparing Native American and First Nations Canadian history and culture with that of the Maori people and found many similarities and common patterns both in the cultural practices and values and in the colonial history.

Following cultural protocols helps to set a relational tone and prepares each person for appropriate interactions. It helps to speed the process along for developing the foundational concept of the importance of seeing each other as relatives. The cultural practices of the Maori and Lakota indigenous people aid in remembering that there is a relational connection to the environment as well as honoring ancestors and acknowledging those yet to come in the future. It is as though they help to establish an understanding that says, "now that we have acknowledged each other as relatives, we can put our minds together to take care of the business at hand."

The reasoning for the importance of following protocols can be found in the words of First Nations Mohawk Elder and scholar Marlene Brandt Castellano reflecting on the opening prayer and acknowledgment protocols of her indigenous Mohawk heritage:

> We start our gatherings acknowledging that we have come from all the directions to be with one another. We come with different lives and experiences, so the process of remembering how we are all related, not only to each other, but also to the plants, creatures, and indeed the entire environment is vital. This takes considerable time but we go through the process led by the Elders. This long protocol ends with leaving us at a place where we can look deep into our hearts to find the finest words possible that express gratitude to the Creator, whose face we cannot see, for giving us good minds to see our way forward.

It is important to note why Jim chose the Native American Ledger Art format for *Blood Warriors*, a piece which won "Best of Show" at a prestigious Native American art show. Ledger Art represents a transitional form of Plains Indian artistry corresponding to the forced reduction of Plains tribes to US government reservations, roughly between 1860 and 1900. Due to the destruction of the buffalo herds and other game animals of the Great Plains by Anglo-Americans during and after the Civil War, paintings on buffalo hide gave way to works on paper, muslin, canvas, and occasionally commercially prepared cow or buffalo hides.

Changes in the content of pictographic art, the rapid adjustment of Plains artists to the relatively small size of a sheet of ledger paper, and the wealth of detail possible with new coloring materials, marks Plains Ledger drawings as a new form of Native American art. As such, Ledger Art portrays a transitional expression of art and material culture that links traditional (pre-reservation) Plains painting to the Plains and Pueblo Indian painting styles that emerged during the 1920s in Indian schools in Oklahoma and New Mexico.

> Beginning in the early 1860s, Plains Indian men adapted their representational style of painting to paper in the form of accountants' ledger books. Traditional paints and bone and stick brushes used to paint on hide gave way to new implements, such as colored pencils, crayons, and occasionally watercolor paints. Plains artists acquired paper and new drawing materials in trade, or as booty after a military engagement, or from a raid. Initially, the content

of Ledger drawings continued the tradition of depicting military exploits and important acts of personal heroism already established in representational painting on buffalo hides and animal skins. As the US government implemented the forced relocation of the Plains peoples to reservations, for all practical purposes completed by the end of the 1870s, Plains artists added scenes of ceremony and daily life from before the reservation to the repertoire of their artwork, reflecting the social and cultural changes brought by life on the reservation within the larger context of forced assimilation (Plains Indian Ledger Art Project).

Just as the backdrop to Jim's art are the numbers, writing, lines, and columns of an accounting ledger, the pervasive influence of colonization and the overwhelming presence of the Western world remain a context for the lives of indigenous peoples the globe over, Lakota, First Nations, Maori, and Pacific Islanders included. The process of colonization includes erasing any trace of the original Peoples off the landscape. It is as if to say the long history of the original People, often thousands of years, is not important and the valued history begins with colonial contact.

Often we rely on—and, at times, look only to—Western concepts and ways of working through our problems and, indeed, of constructing our lives. Ledger Art is a metaphor for what Jim and I are trying to express here and for our experience during this trip. In fact, it can be seen as a metaphor for how we have chosen to live our lives and how we view the world. Even though we move through, engage, and are immersed in the Western world, making our way as best as we can, we also strive to restore and incorporate indigenous ways of being, overlaying the Western world with the beauty, genius, and brilliance of ancient indigenous ways.

The metaphor that can be found within Ledger Art is also a metaphor for the Ruth Yellowhawk Fellowship research reported on here. It is an attempt to take several steps back, much as we do in order to enjoy a painting or other artistic expression in its entirety. It is an attempt to articulate a scene rather than to describe the process details. It is like ascending a mountain or other high place to observe the lay of the land, the winding of the rivers, where the forests, plains, and marshes begin and end; it notices the creatures and people within the scene. It is about telling the story that emerged naturally.

References

Manahi, G. "Downgrading of Haane Manahi's Victoria Cross." 1998. Retrieved from: http://eng.kiamau.tki.org.nz/Multimedia/Company-B/Downgrading-of-Haane-Manahi-s-Victoria-Cross (accessed Aug. 3, 2015).

Plains Indian Ledger Art Project. University of California, San Diego Department of Ethnic Studies, 2013, https://plainsledgerart.org/history (accessed Aug. 3, 2015).

Harley Eagle is of the Dakota/Anishinabe First Nations, enrolled in the Whitecap Dakota First Nations Reserve, in Saskatchewan, Canada. Eagle is a long-time practitioner of Restorative Justice and Mediation, assisting individuals and groups to work through conflict. He is the co-coordinator of Indigenous Work for Mennonite Central Committee Canada and serves as the co-chair of the KAIROS Indigenous Rights Circle.

7

Strategies for Creating a Friendly Environment in an Unfriendly World

A Comparative Study of Ethnic Tensions in Russia and the United States

by
Alina Starinets

In present-day Russia, as in the United States, racial and ethnic tensions affect certain groups of people, who continue to be targets of discrimination, both economically and socially. Many people in both countries live on the margins of existence, excluded from the mainstream development process. Inequality continues to be a major problem in both societies and tends to reproduce itself over time. If full ethnic and racial equality seems an unattainable utopia in the contemporary world, are there at least ways in which we can move in the right direction? Practicing tolerance is the answer that comes to mind. The concept of "tolerance" however, should not be thought of as a synonym for avoidance or meekness in the larger society. Rather, it implies an active bilateral process requiring efforts from both minorities and local residents. In order to interact constructively with someone from a completely different background, one must first reassess one's own identity and values. A society without clear ideas about its own citizenship will fail to inspire others to perceive themselves as full-fledged citizens. Hosting societies shouldn't treat immigration and migration as something inevitable, but rather try to enjoy it as a unique opportunity for self-introspection and reflection.

Critical judgment about one's own traditions is the first step. As the poet T.S. Eliot observed: "I doubt whether a poet or novelist can be universal without being local too," so only those who are well aware of their own cultural traditions can move beyond them and only those who understand where the boundaries are, can overstep them. But if the first step is to reassess oneself and to show respect for what may seem strange, where do the limits of tolerance lie? As playwright John Doble says, "it depends."

Will there be a day when Russia and the United States will be proud of their citizens with a wide variety of ethnic backgrounds or will minorities continue to remain patchworks of closed ethnic communities? The fact that people make efforts to shut themselves off from the wider environment is not the sign of a healthy democratic society. Those from different backgrounds can be welcomed and integrated only by a society with a strong culture of citizenship. According to sociological theory, the concept of citizenship is usually low in countries with a totalitarian past. The main thing about citizenship is a feeling that needs to have been accumulated through several generations.

What does it means to be a citizen? What is one's true identity? Although these questions seem, at first glance, only tangentially connected to the problem of ethnic inequality, they are, in fact, the key paths to its solution.

A Brief Outline of Migration in Contemporary Russia

Compared to Americans, Russians treat the history of immigration in their country with considerably less reverence. Despite a long history of great human migration (including the Mongol-Tatar invasion of Russia [Rus'] in the 13th century, and the Volga Germans, who moved to Russia under the rule of Catherine the Great in the 18th century), Russians tended to ignore the whole issue until the collapse of the Soviet Union in 1991. (The Soviet Union was, by its very nature, a forced mix of nations, officially proclaimed as "Unity for Friendship.") The largest flow of migrants Russia has ever experienced has occurred in the last 20 years, leaving locals in a state of shock, which soon turned to frustration and anger. Twenty years turned out not to be enough to deal with this in any useful way while in the meantime the flow of migrants from the former Soviet republics into Russia not only has not decreased, but has increased in volume.

The main reason for the migration lies in the economies of former Soviet republics, which did not recover after the USSR collapse, when poverty emerged and became widespread. An abrupt widening of the gap between the economies and social care system of oil-rich Russia and those of its former republics, stimulated people to look for jobs in Russia. *Guestarbeiter*, a term of German origin, enriched Russian vocabulary and came into popular usage. It has a sad (and often humiliating) connotation primarily implying a migrant worker, employed in low-paid work (often illegally) and accommodated in inhumane conditions, which do not differ that much from the ones in concentration camps. Moreover, in the mind of an average Russian, the notion of "migrant" has been perverted to mean something similar to *guestarbeiter*, symbolically representing an Asian-looking person from the "five-stan countries" (Tajikistan being the poorest among the former Soviet republics) who is sweeping streets in Moscow.

The jobs migrants pursue in Russia, the most menial and lowest paid, are not popular among locals. It's obviously not competition for jobs that is the real cause of tension. So why do local Russian residents look with more favor on Ukrainians or Byelorussians, who also come to Russia as job seekers and are far more likely to compete for higher positions, the ones that locals strive for as well? Is it because of the disparities of appearance between Asians and so-called "white Russians"? Or does the reason for this latent xenophobia among Russians lie deeper in their mentalities, in a subconscious assumption that a different-looking person is more likely to be of another religion, namely Islam, the religion of the majority of Tajiks, Uzbeks, Turkmens, and Kyrgyz people and half of the Kazakh people? If these deeply held prejudices are indeed at work, the attempts of the Russian government to update labor law regarding migrants will not eliminate ethnic conflicts entirely.

One of the main characteristics of this post-Soviet flow of migrants into Russia is its unequal spread. It tends to be very much centralized: the majority of people go to Moscow. Increasing the population density in Moscow contributes to tension in the city. Municipal authorities estimate that the total number of illegal migrants is between 200,000 and 300,000 people. Despite this fact, Moscow's government, has persisted in its policy of restricting quotas for hiring migrant workers in recent years, with the result of increasing the ranks of the so-called "invisible men." People from the former Soviet republics usually do not require visas to Russia, so they come legally and then, because of the existing labor laws, which are highly criminalized, they are forced to move into the shadows. Instead of putting all their efforts into finding and deporting illegal migrants, the authorities need to begin targeting cheating employers.

Some steps have already been taken in this direction. In 2013, the government adopted a law, requiring all employers hiring migrants to provide them with health benefits. It is also now considering an offer to provide support for migrants before they migrate, by introducing special governmental migration consultants based in their home countries. It often turns out that people arrive in Russia utterly unprepared for life in a new country, with no idea what to expect. The government should also think about opening the so-called "closed lists," containing data of migrants who are for some reason unwelcome in Russia. Now it often happens that such migrants arrive at Russian border control posts and only there learn that their names are "on the lists," that they have to go back home and that they have spent all their money for travel in vain. The majority of such people are poor, and in order to make the trip to Russia, they run into debt, owing money to all their relatives and friends. The defense of human rights of migrants lies in details—as they say, great acts are made up of small deeds. Instead of hunting for illegal workers, one should have a better look at the way the social care system is provided to them. For instance, at present, the transfer of retirement money from Russia to another country is not well developed and gives migrants lots of headaches.

Despite the fact that many more migrants live in Moscow than the comparative few who find their way to remote rural areas, the likelihood of a peaceful solution to the problem still favors this huge historically cosmopolitan city. It's easier to be an alien and interact with strangers in a big city with its high level of anonymity and superficial contacts than to adapt to a smaller community with its own traditions, neighborhood control, and approval. It is a sort of optimistic forecast, that at least in Moscow the problems of ethnic tension will be easier to handle. The reality is that in recent years the worst ethnic riots, which can be labeled as nationalist-based violence, took place both in Moscow and in the small town of Kondopoga in Karelia, the northwestern part of Russia. In both cases, the mass violence was fueled by a casual incident—a quarrel in a restaurant in Kondopoga, when three Russians offended an Azerbaijani waiter who was serving them, and at a bus stop in Moscow, where a Russian football fan quarreled with a Kabardino Balkarian from the North Caucasus. Both cases ended in gunfights and homicides. TV coverage of those crimes subsequently spurred unprecedented riots by Russian nationals involving 2,000 people in Kondopoga and 5,000 in Moscow. Since then the name of

Kondopoga has become notorious in Russia and is often used as a definition for any ethnic conflict taking place anywhere in the country.

A modern post-script to be noted is that calls for such riots, especially in Moscow, which is fully Internet equipped, are usually spread via Internet. The Russian Special Police troops feel awkward when suddenly they find they have to fight 12- or 13-year-olds. It's kids who have primarily invaded the Internet and represent the most hypnotizable stratum of society. Thus, the riot that took place in Moscow in June 2012 (it also started from refusal to share a table in a cafe) even got a medieval name: "Children's Crusade."

Another peculiarity is that, in contemporary Russia, immigration doesn't mean the intention of settling for good as is often the case in the United States, where immigrants usually come to stay forever. In Russia, migrants primarily work in shifts, going back and forth from their native countries to Russia. So patterns of immigration here resemble a sort of human circulation, pumping through economically successful regions (namely through Russia, which is one of the most industrialized and economically prosperous of the former Soviet republics). People come in order to make some money and go back home. And insofar as most of the migrants do not consider Russia as their future home, it often leads to a careless attitude towards the Russian environment, which increases ethnic tension.

Still, the wish to come to work only for a shift should not lead to setting up ghettos for migrants, as was considered in October 2012. Driven by the notion of isolating migrants from the local environment, the Public Chamber of the Russian Federation took the creation of such ghettos under consideration. Supporters of the idea stated that the founding of these kinds of "labor camps," as they called them, would enable the government to save money. They would not have to invest in Russian language classes for migrants or in other measures designed to adapt them to the new environment. This issue evoked heated debates both in the Chamber and in the society. Fortunately, the idea did not find favor. The majority were of the opinion that migrants should not be isolated from society, but rather should get support in adapting to the Russian environment. Most also felt that local Russian residents should try to adapt to the more ethnically diverse environment, which now attracts lots of people of other nations.

It should be noted that migration from former Soviet republics to Russia didn't begin in the 1990s; Georgians, Armenians, and Azerbaijanis began migrating to Russia in the 1970s. The immigration that occurred between 1970 and 1990, however, was of a very different character from that which emerged from the collapse of the Soviet Union. Not only were there many fewer immigrants in the earlier period but it was, for the most part, their intention to settle in Russia permanently. The descendants of those early ethnic settlers are now deeply rooted in Russia, often occupying high-level professional jobs that require a good education. These immigrants are more inclined to identify themselves as Russians, than as representatives of ethnic minorities. And they tend to reveal almost the same degree of intolerance towards newly arrived migrants, as other Russians do.

Present-day migrants seem to represent one of the most vulnerable, underprivileged strata of society, the victims of various kinds of injustice, extremism, and xenophobia. At the same time, it is often their own behavior and patterns of life that frustrate Russians and fuel the ethnic tensions. For instance, Russians are maddened by the way the Caucasians drive. Caucasians often violate speed limits and do not observe traffic laws, as they used to do in their own countries. There is even a special slang for these drivers—*dzhigitovka*, a derivative from the Caucasian word *dzhigit*, a term similar to "cowboy." Another growing problem concerns migrants from former Asian republics, like Kazakhstan, which is now notorious for human trafficking and slavery. Upon investigating cases of slavery in Russian territory, police in most cases find that the culprits are not Russian, but representatives of former Soviet republics who are keeping their own compatriots as slaves.

According to researchers, Russia currently maintains a workable interethnic balance and is ready to absorb more migrants from decaying post-Soviet republics. But socioeconomic conditions can change any time. For instance, now the average migrant is a young man at the height of his productive power, who comes without his family. He works shifts and regularly goes back to his homeland. When or if migrants begin bringing their wives, children, and elderly relatives to Russia with them, the existing socioeconomic balance may well change for the worse. On the other hand, living with their families might improve the attitudes and behavior of migrants because it is likely that loneliness and the lack of familiar surroundings and people is at the root of many crimes committed by migrants.

One more thing is the current proportion of nationals in the territory of Russia. For instance, Armenians and Azerbaijanis, who are currently living in Russia, find it a comfortable country attractive for living in. But this of its low-income, often minority, residents. New residents, the so-called "urban pioneers" are usually educated, well-to-do, and predominantly white.

Though forcing a blended society is a social utopia, there do exist some examples of its efficient implementation. In Zurich, Switzerland, as well as in some other places in Western Europe, local authorities have introduced settlement quotas, and all the legally arriving immigrants are offered a choice of districts where they can settle, based on the current proportion of nationalities already in residence in those neighborhoods. It's one efficient way of breaking segregated housing patterns. The forced social interaction between people of widely differing backgrounds gradually leads to strengthening their relationships, as generalized views of an anonymous ethnic group shift to interactions on an individual level.

In contemporary Russia the situation is reversed: the main source of information about where to settle comes to migrants from their relatives or acquaintances, who have moved to Russia before them. And that cannot but lead to ghetto-type settlements. Such kinds of "shadow cities," do not lead to integration but rather to avoidance, which can be peaceful only up to a point. Clashes are inevitable.

Placing people of different ethnicities side by side is one of the main means of overcoming the fears and insecurities of both sides. Research shows that people who have friends or acquaintances among immigrants, display a positive attitude towards immigration. Programs that welcome immigrants can be found around the world. Immigrant students in 14 US states pay significantly less tuition in public colleges; in Vancouver, Canada, volunteers provide a number of adult programs and services to immigrants. Belfast, Ireland, offers floating clinics, trade union support of migrant workers, and other integration initiatives while Bilbao, Spain, sponsors a number of successful programs that promote the social inclusion of migrants.

The workplace is where adults share common interests and spend most of their time. Therefore projects that welcome the hiring of employees of various ethnicities and social status, play a crucial role in decreasing ethnic tension and uniting people living in the same area. Kolomna, a small town near Moscow, provides a good example. In addition to reviving the local tradition of producing marshmallow sticks, which made that town famous during Soviet times, the current owners of the factory promote the idea of equal-opportunity employment offering work to migrants, retired people, and various other underpriviledged groups. Of course, they have to pass a trial period successfully, after which—if they verify their loyalty—they get the job.

Urban vs. Rural

Modern city dwellers tend to cherish their personal autonomy and seldom have strong ties in the community around them. The ties within communities of small towns and especially rural areas, on the other hand, are as strong as they have ever been. Thus, it seems obvious, that approaches to the adaptation of migrants and immigrants in each of these cases should be different.

While community still remains the cornerstone in rural areas and small towns, in big cities the social ties have gradually frayed with little else to take their place. But even urban people need a sense of community. So the answer, in urban areas, is smart planning of public spaces.

Of course, planners cannot solve this problem alone—the social environment, including schools and job markets must change as well. Creative people, like artists, writers, and entrepreneurs should be invited to rethink ways to strengthen relationships in cities. An example of such fruitful cooperation can be found in Cincinnati, Ohio, where authorities conduct the so-called "graffiti celebrations." As in many US cities, the middle-class residents of Cincinnati have left downtown for the suburbs. As a result the city's public spaces are no longer well maintained. In order to revive them, local authorities, in collaboration with artists, began promoting "graffiti weekends," inviting residents of all social strata to enjoy graffiti being painted in their presence and thus killing two birds with one stone: refreshing the look of the city and at the same time bringing life back to downtown and mixing its residents of different social class and ethnicity.

The "Welcome Dayton" Initiative

Dayton, Ohio, situated at the intersection of major north-south and east-west interstate highways has always been a busy city. Once a thriving auto manufacturing center, the city suffered considerable economic devastation as a result of the Great Recession. It is confronted now with the challenge of reinventing itself. One of the strategies is to become an immigrant-friendly city and to promote a positive approach to integrating immigrants into the community. This initiative was given the name "Welcome Dayton." Then-Dayton-mayor Gary Leitzell defined what the city needs most for recovery: "more community involvement, a more loving attitude toward one another, and an attitude of togetherness. Immigrants are the greatest assets of this community."

Development of such policies means that people are now ready to move past the days of treating immigrants as second-class citizens and criminals. But building community among neighbors in a city that suffers from segregation and alienation is, of course, a challenging task. Change doesn't come overnight, and there is still tension about newly arriving immigrants.

Conducting open dialogues between immigrant advocates and city officials is an important step in developing the initiative. It shifted the debate from "they take our jobs" to an "asset-based community-building model." Denying immigrants the opportunity to integrate incurs public costs, such as homelessness and crime.

The Welcome Dayton plan positions this Rust Belt city to become a competitor in the global economy by "attracting the best and the brightest" from around the world and encouraging them to start new businesses in Dayton.

Signs of moving in a positive direction include activities, such as Dayton World Soccer Games (the tournament includes residents of all ages and backgrounds), a Hike for Health initiative and Hound Hikes, Pioneer Woman: Quilting conducted at Grant Park, Adult Nature Discovery Walks and Butterfly Monitoring, Family Camping, and summer tennis leagues. All these projects are aimed at bringing people together so they can get to know each other as individuals. When people become your friends and you know their families, you don't want them to be deported. That is the human essence of the Welcome Dayton project.

Museums

Current activities in American museums that promote the ideas of equality and rights for migrants set a good example for their colleagues from all over the world. One vivid example of such a cultural contribution was a 2013 exhibition at the Art Institute of Chicago entitled, "They Seek a City: Chicago and the Art of Migration 1910-1950." Particular attention in the Chicago exhibition was devoted to Mexican modernism, which had a great influence on the artistic life in Chicago. It showed progressive, socially concerned American artists, a crucial model for the political impact of art, and created a fertile exchange between two cultures. On the whole, the personal migration experiences of the artists provided a creative tool for their appeal for social justice. The sober social realism reflected in their art spoke to a deeper truth of life. These artists took to heart the importance of exposing the inequalities faced by oppressed minority groups.

Historically, Chicago has been one of the nation's most attractive cities for migrants. Today it hosts one of the biggest Latin American communities in the United States. Presenting art works in which migrants are portrayed with empathy and dignity helps to reassure the broader community that newly arriving immigrants share the same moral values and will be able to adjust to American life.

Schools

For schools, of course, facilitating positive change is part of their mission in bringing up children as responsible citizens. One can safely say that schools are the ideal place for children of different ethnicities to relate to each other in a natural way.

It is obvious that mixing helps children get on in life. In the 1960s, the United States undertook racial desegregation in its public schools, largely by means of bussing children from one school district to another to achieve diversity. Mandatory school bussing was not without its successes, but it left a great many problems in its wake. There continue to be major inequities between school districts in poorer areas (often populated by immigrants and other minorities) and schools in well-to-do, largely white, communities.

Russia does not have such a problem. Children of different ethnic groups usually study together. The main problem here is that the Ministry for Education has not established any standards-based programs to help migrant children adapt to the new culture in which they find themselves. On the other hand, some excellent local programs do exist. One such, called "World without Boundaries" was implemented at Secondary School #384 in Moscow by its deputy director, Elena Kurashkina. The school is located in a low-income district that is home to various ethnic groups. In its classrooms, one can sometimes find children of some 38 different ethnicities. The main three goals of this program, according to its founder, are to:

- facilitate the mastery of Russian language skills;
- promote tolerance in children from the host community; and
- support the development of personal identity and character in the children of migrants.

The first step Kurashkina took in introducing her new program to the school staff was to send all the Russian language teachers to sharpen their skills at the Moscow Institute of Open Education. She also hired more psychologists specializing in the social adaptation problems and identity crises experienced by migrants, she brought bilingual language experts on board, and she opened a new position for a teacher specializing in patriotic upbringing.

Program activities were built around the idea of preserving memories of World War II. It was during that time that Soviet people of many different nationalities fought together, side by side; many contemporary children are the descendants of those soldiers. So she invited her students to join the International Association of Scouts aimed at preserving memories of war veterans and searching for the relatives of those who perished. To enhance the patriotic work in this project she organized student volunteers to support the veterans of the Defense of Brest Fortress (a battle that symbolized Soviet resistance to the Nazi invasion). She also invited children to join the international movement "Kind Children of the World" and is now hosting interregional meetings at the school. Many other activities, such as volunteer clean-ups of the local area, ecological activities like tree planting or feeding birds in winter, various competitions such as a "Best Reciter" contest, and establishment of a school theater studio and a school hiking club, are regularly available to children in this program as well.

A critical aspect of the deputy director's reform project was the special attention given to raising students' awareness of legislative issues. In a class, entitled "Law and Order," students discuss xenophobia, neofascism, and other kinds of radical movements. She also carefully introduced religious studies, making them nonobligatory and covering not only Orthodox Christianity but also the basics of all major religions of the world.

Finally, Kurashkina defined indices—such as the number of migrants' children with a positive attitude towards studying and the number of migrant parents participating actively in the school lives of their children— to measure change and evaluate the success of the program.

Libraries

Libraries are no longer mere storage spaces for information. In much of the contemporary world, libraries actively promote themselves as attractive public spaces, where people meet for a variety of educational and civic purposes. This movement has been gaining momentum in Russia as well. With regard to reducing ethnic tension, the School of Migrants project at the Gorky Library in Perm, Russia, is the first initiative of its kind in the country. The program is quite intense—classes meet three times a week and last for four hours. For reasons unknown, of all the ethnic groups currently living in the area, Tajiks turned out to be the most active participants. The main aim of the project is elimination of legal, psychological, language, and other barriers migrants encounter in their host country. In addition to conducting classes, the Gorky Library compiled lists of local organizations that are most likely to provide advice or jobs to migrants. The Perm School of Migrants project is supported by local authorities, thanks to the efforts of the library staff.

APPENDIX
Focus Group Questionnaire and Results

The participants chosen for the focus group were a homogenous group (all well-educated Russians, all in approximately the same age range (30-45), and all employed in public centers (libraries and nonprofit organizations) and thus, presumably, like-minded, with a more than average openness of mind regarding ethnic tensions issue. The group contained both male and female participants with a slight male predominance.

Therefore, the main weakness of this focus group was that it didn't convey the opinions of representatives of other nations of the former Soviet Union, primarily, the so-called five-stan republics: Kazakhstan, Kyrgyzstan, Turkmenistan, Uzbekistan, and Tajikistan. With the collapse of the Soviet Union, post-Soviet republics situated in Asia have become the poorest states, supplying contemporary Russia with a cheap workforce, both legal and illegal.

1. In your perception, has the general state of ethnic relations in Russia changed (for the worse or for the better) within the last five years? Explain why you think so.

The youngest person stated that the situation had definitely changed for the worse, because of the illegal immigrant flow and the fact that no coherent practices have been developed to prevent it. The feedback from older people was less harsh; one even stated, that ethnic relations are now changing for the better. One person

9. *Do you support or oppose the following? (Support/Oppose/Unsure)–continued*

Requiring visas for migrants from the former Soviet republics so they can be protected and at the same time controlled	Only one participant opposed this idea, while others split between "support" and "unsure." It should be noted that requiring such visas would certainly become an additional obstacle for representatives of poor countries seeking jobs in Russia.
Providing support for migrants before they migrate, through governmental migration consultants based in their home country	Half of the participants supported this idea, while others either opposed it or were unsure. The reason for such a cautious attitude might lie in the fact that such organizations would likely have to be funded by Russian money.
Hiring legal migrants (medical insurance, social support provided by the employer, etc.) and facilitating conditions for migrant-friendly organizations (quotas for foreign labor migrants, etc.)/ strengthening legal punishments against companies taking advantage of employing illegal migrants	All the participants shared the view that migrants need social support provided by their Russian employers, but one of the participants still specified that such measures should be introduced only after all local Russians start enjoying such benefits.
Strengthening legal punishments against companies taking advantage of employing illegal migrants	Everybody supported this idea.
Introducing age limitations for the migrants (If yes—what would be the age?)	One participant not only supported the idea of setting an age limitation for migrants, but suggested narrowing it severely to a range between 20 and 25.

(continued on next page)

9. *Do you support or oppose the following? (Support/Oppose/Unsure)—continued*

Insisting that migrants deposit an amount of money with the RF government, thus introducing financial responsibility for migrants upon their arrival. It would serve as a sort of financial cushion to be used for their deportation in case they committed crimes, or needed some complicated surgery or other medical services.	More than one-half of the participants supported this idea. One was opposed, and one was unsure. The tricky point here is that the majority of migrants going to work in Russia are poor, and it's often a challenge for them to save money even for their travel tickets. Requiring the additional expense of a deposit would provide yet another obstacle in the way of their earning money in Russia.
Introducing special labor camps (reservation areas) for temporary migrant guest workers (the proposal in the Public Chamber of RF in 2012)	It was amazing to me that one of the participants supported the idea of "special labor camps." That was actually a trick question that I thought no one would consider seriously. Another person in the group did not reject the idea at first but seriously considered it from the point of its efficiency. Ultimately he rejected it on the grounds that it would be inefficient in practice; according to him, such measures only cause protest and encourage immigration, as had been shown when tried in other countries.
Including ethnic profiling in police investigations	More than one-half of the participants supported the idea, while the rest remained unsure. On the one hand, emphasizing nationality in most cases has nothing to do with the crime committed by the individual. On the other hand, in the case of terrorist attacks, the nationality issue might be crucial.

10. Would you disapprove if your child's partner belonged to another nation (Central Asian, former Soviet republics, etc.)

It was no wonder that the same participants who favored introducing age limitation and reservation areas (labor camps) in previous questions, were against their children being involved in interethnic marriages.

11. Do you know anyone in an interethnic relationship?

Almost all the participants answered "yes" to this question.

12. How does your ethnic (Russian) identity influence the way you see the world?

The majority of the participants stated that their Russian nationality didn't influence their identity, while one emphasized the large contribution of the Russian nation in the areas of arts, education, etc. and his own feeling of connection to it.

13. Is your feeling of patriotism somehow connected with your ethnic identity?

The majority answered "no."

14. To what extent does the national identity of other people shape the way you see them? Does knowing someone's nationality—for instance, Georgian or Armenian, Tajikistani or Kazakhstani—immediately tell you something about a person?

One person narrowed this question to Islam vs. Christianity. Another admitted that there are some general clichés in his mind. A third person also said that he has some stereotypes. He said he tries to ignore them but they still emerged subconsciously. Others stated that the preliminary knowledge of someone's national identity did not influence their judgment on the person at all.

15. Do you think that representatives of some specific nationality tend to be more dangerous or criminal (or wealthy, or hardworking, or uneducated) than others? Are there general conceptions about particular nationalities that are now settled in Russia?

This question echoes the previous one. The participants who tended to operate with stereotypes in their minds, specified here, that Asians are more effective workers and less criminal than Caucasians.

16. Do you observe migrant clusters in Moscow? Do you see a problem with this?

The majority of the participants answered "yes" to both questions.

17. Is the term *migrant* a synonym for *guest worker* to you?

The participants were split evenly on this question, so the perception of the term by Russians remains unclear.

18. What do you think is the primary cause of ethnic tensions in Russia?

Illegal immigration; lack of education and disrespectful behavior (violations of cultural codes on both sides). The person, who had previously stated that he tries to fight against nationalistic stereotypes that occur in his mind subconsciously, here extended his own problem to the level of the whole Russian society. He also stated that it's only migrants who are disrespectful, not the locals.

19. What are the greatest challenges to improving ethnic relations in Russia?

Inconsistency in the federal law; low cultural level of people and their intolerance in general; poverty and social insecurity. The person who was negative on the issue in most questions, here offered legal restrictions for migrants and introducing visas with former Soviet republics.

20. Have you ever witnessed ethnic tension? (What happened? Who was the victim? Who was the perpetrator? Was there a mediator?)

Two of the participants stated that they hadn't witnessed any real ethnic conflict. The rest provided examples, such as disorders resulting from Kurban Bayrami celebrations, when Muslims slaughter sheep in public in the streets of Russian cities, and an instance when unpaid Tajik workers, cheated by their employer, rioted.

21. In your opinion, where does ethnic discrimination reveal its highest level?
- while being interviewed for a job
- while renting an apartment
- while arranging official documents
- other

One person did not fill in the chart, but wrote that one should mark all the options and that the reason for such discrimination lies primarily in the misbehavior of young migrants, specifically citing their picking up Russian girls for sex. He added that they shouldn't dare to do that because "they have nothing to offer them due to their low education and bad manners."

22. What role do civic NGOs play in the migrant issue in Russia?

One person stated that presently the NGOs are weak and play a minimal role, while the key actors now are media, schools, and pop culture. Others saw NGOs as mediators and providers of space where ethnic tensions and problems can be discussed.

23. What is the role of Western funding in helping NGOs finance solutions to Russian migration problems?

One person stated that Russians should be capable of solving their own problems, and that the less Western money is involved, the better. Another one added, that efficiencies offered by Western money decrease in the Russian environment. Others see nothing bad in spending Western money on research and other projects.

References

Alexeev, Mikhail. *Immigration Phobia and the Security Dilemma: Russia, Europe and the United States*. Cambridge University Press, 2006.

Centerville-Washington Park District. www.cwpd.org/news4.html (accessed July 19, 2015).

Florida, Richard. *The Rise of the Creative Class*. New York: Perseus Book Group, 2002.

Glass, Ruth. *London: Aspects of Change*. London: Centre for Urban Studies, 1964.

Glazytchev, Vyatcheslav. *Development Nowadays and in the Past*.

Guiso, Luigi, Paola Sapienza, and Luigi Zingales. *Social Capital as Good Culture*. National Bureau of Economic Research, 2007, www.nber.org/papers/w13712 (accessed July 19, 2015).

Hartigan, Jr., John. *Racial Situations: Class Predicaments of Whiteness in Detroit*. Princeton, NJ: Princeton University Press, 1999.

Jacobs, Jane. *The Death and Life of Great American Cities*. New York: Random House, 1961.

Landry, Charles. *The Creative City: A Toolkit for Urban Innovators*. New York, NY: Routledge, 2008.

Morones, Enrique. *The Power of One. The Story of the Border Angels*. San Diego State University Press, 2012.

Mamford, Lewis. *The Myth of the Machine: Technics and Human Development*. New York: Mariner Books, 1971.

A New Path toward a Humane Immigration Policy. American Friends Service Committee, 2013, www.afsc.org/documents/new-path-full-version (accessed July 19, 2015).

Park, Robert Ezra. *The City as Social Laboratory*. University of Chicago Press, 1929.

Patchenkov, Oleg. *Mobility and Excessive Use of Publicity*.

Policy Studies Institute. "Case Study of Manchester." http://www.psi.org.uk/publications/archivepdfs/Profitable/BIC9.pdf (accessed Aug. 9, 2015).

Ravinsky, D. "Library and Challenges of the XXI Century," 2010.

Rivera, Geraldo. *His Panic: Why Americans Fear Hispanics in the U.S.* New York: Celebra, 2008.

Scheffer, Paul. *Immigrant Nations.* Cambridge: Polity Press, 2011.

Zamyatina, N., and A. Ilyasov. *Russia That We Acquired: Studying Space at Microlevel.* New Chronograph, 2013.

A native of Moscow, Alina Starinets is an international relations officer at the All-Russia State Library for Foreign Literature. With an educational background in theater and English language studies, she has worked for many years as a writer, editor, and translator for a variety of media and other Russian companies.

8

Cross-Cultural Management of International Education

by
Zhang Chunping

Part One: Cross-Cultural Management of International Education

International education programs at the School of International Studies of Peking University (PKU) have grown rapidly since 2006, and the demand for building an effective, multiculturally capable team to administer international education is increasing. Instances of misunderstanding and miscommunication have occurred during the past seven years as we have moved toward a more consolidated international education program. Cultural discomfort and uneasiness between collaborators from different cultural backgrounds impede our endeavors to further improve internationalization at Peking University.

My research on cross-cultural management in international education is aimed at finding ways to ease these discomforts, enhance the cross-cultural competency of our administration, and integrate my experiences and analysis into our training and team-building programs. Based on my academic exchange trips to a few American universities and institutions, I have learned the following points that could enhance the effectiveness of the international education administration at PKU.

The Need for Pre-orientation Preparation

Line Lillevick, program director for the dual-degree program in International and World History offered by the London School of Economics and the history department of Columbia University, admits that first-year international students at Columbia who come from European countries often settle into American culture more easily than those from Asia. It may take Asian students months to keep up with their classes and academic research and feel comfortable mingling in the local culture. Conversely, Lillevick said she could easily imagine the culture shock for Western students when they first land in China for an academic year packed with intensive coursework and a dissertation to finish. She suggests that we should try to address the cultural differences before students even set off for China.

For the new cohort coming to PKU in late August or early September, it is important to increase their awareness of life and cultural conditions in the country where they will live, well in advance of their arrival. The program advisors should be in frequent communication with the new cohort members, advising them of essentials regarding social, religious, and legal aspects of life in China, as well as academic requirements, calendars, and schedules. A university orientation book containing general information about campus life should also be provided to the new members, so that they have a more thorough understanding of what to expect during their one or two years at PKU.

To establish a network, the PKU international education administration can connect the new cohort with the senior cohorts on a "Book with Faces" (Facebook is not available in mainland China). In 2011, this social network also proved to be very effective in finding housing for the new cohort. It is important that we provide a complete profile book of our faculty members to the new students so that they may explore the research fields of our respective faculty members and build contacts early for seeking advice. We should also make sure inquiries from the new students are addressed in a responsive manner over the summer break, which begins in July.

Providing Cultural Essentials during Orientation

The orientation week on campus should be instructive and informative to help incoming international students properly choose and register their courses and to build a sense of comfort in the context of the local culture. The orientation program should be reinforced with additional cultural content and students should be guided carefully through possible initial stages of anxiety, suspicion, antagonism, or even defiance of the local culture and rules. We should be sensitive to such emotions and reactions when students first arrive; then we need to show them the importance and benefits of being a responsible foreigner in this country.

David Bronkema, director of international development programs at Eastern University, points out that we should welcome the international students with a very open attitude, encouraging them to ask cultural questions in addition to guiding them through setting up their coursework and collecting the required reading packets. His words inspired me with the idea of sketching a comic book that contains simple but direct information to help foreign students observe Chinese culture, using humor to list "things to avoid." Or we could orchestrate a comedy show for the new cohort, put on by the senior international students along with Chinese students, to illustrate a possible collision of different cultures.

Hildy Heath, director of the Office of International Programs at San Francisco State University, believes educators should not consider bending some rules for international students to make them feel more comfortable. She thinks the international students should be treated equally with the local students, with no exception. That's the way standards are properly kept.

Methodology and research tools should be provided to the international students to facilitate their understanding of the local culture. The deliberation tools I learned at Kettering Foundation could be used to inspire students in finding and framing their issues. Their questions and concerns could then be dealt with in a deliberative manner. The second tool I suggest is the Iceberg Model, which stresses the importance of observing the larger—yet sometimes hidden—part of a culture that lies beneath the surface.

Taking international students on tours of the city and the communities around the university will help build their initial sense of daily life in China and help them to explore the local mentality, ethics, and social dynamics. We could also encourage the Chinese students, who usually comprise as much as 30 percent of the cohort, to help the international students not only as language study partners, but also in guiding their efforts to observe the local culture and rules, including values and ethics, people's behaviors, emotions, interpersonal relations, family structure, kinship, societal issues, collective traumas, and so forth. James Cook at UNC Charlotte supports my ideas to increase the cultural content of our orientation at PKU. He believes it is equally important to emphasize the students' social responsibilities in their new environment.

An orientation with our partner school should take place shortly after PKU's orientation week, giving the new cohort a way of seeing life at two institutions as a whole, instead of just looking at the program in a divided way. This will contribute to students making a relatively consistent academic schedule for the entire program of study.

Sharing Ideas for Performance

To encourage two-way communication with the students and instructors, PKU faculty should monitor the students' performance—both in their coursework and class interactions—and share the data with our partner school administration. Program advisors should meet with the class once every two weeks as a mechanism for collecting feedback information. Their opinions could be framed and reflected in a deliberative way to help instructors further fine-tune their class dynamics and improve teaching-learning results.

Anonymous Evaluation

We should allow the students to write anonymous evaluations (questionnaires) towards the end of each semester, creating an open opportunity for students to really pour out their thoughts about their life and education at PKU. They could reflect on the courses they have taken in terms of teaching quality and teaching methods, as well as other aspects of the program. The results should be compared and taken under serious consideration before being shared with the program instructors. The evaluation results will be a resource to help our administrators further improve the quality of the program.

Alumni Work

We should follow the careers or continuing studies of graduates of the program, which could help to further evaluate the long-term effectiveness of our educational courses and program as a whole. By continuing to solicit views and suggestions from program graduates, we will get a sense of their experiences in China, as well as the lasting effects of the international education program on their lives, which will, in turn, help us further improve our curriculum and procedures.

Make It Organic

Compared to the pattern of China's development so far, which has been primarily based on high investment, high consumption, and high pollution, we can make our educational program more "organic" by focusing on the *people* who run and contribute to the program. We should not merely teach in English, but educate our people more effectively about the many facets of education and life in the world outside of China before we hope to boost our programs to the next level of international competency. It will not happen overnight.

It is in the spirit of this cross-cultural awareness that I include my own observations as an international student from China living in the United States.

Part Two: My Cultural Observations in the United States

It is actually very hard for me to define this part of my research in the United States. I initially wanted to explore public attitudes in the United States toward China's "rise." However, I found myself contemplating a bigger question that has long been a debate among some of China's intellectuals: is the United States of America still a melting pot, or (as suggested by Samuel Huntington in *The Clash of Civilizations*) after the 9/11 attack, is the United States just a mosaic picture of its people from more than 250 ethnic backgrounds, subject to an easily triggered collapse?

In methodology, I've been very much inspired by Francis L. K. Hsu's[1] research on how cultures and human behaviors use the advanced tool of "psychosocial homeostasis."[2] Hsu was born in China, educated in Europe, and became an American citizen in the 1940s. He believed that "personality is a Western concept rooted in individualism. The basic importance accorded it in psychological anthropology has obscured our understanding of how Western man lives in Western society and culture, or how any man lives in any society and culture. What is missing is the central ingredient in the human mode of existence: man's relationship with his fellow men."[3]

I was eager to explore the real-world scenarios and dynamics that explain how Americans as a nation share a value system that encourages immigrants from all over the world to recognize themselves as "Americans." In China, citizens struggle hard to find a path to appropriately identify themselves as "Chinese." The cultural lineage of China has been widely considered broken for some years, resulting in a massive loss of the traditional values that used to bond people together in a national identity. How do immigrants settle and strive to make better lives in the United States and how do they retain their cultural personalities in this country with its greater national mentality? Do they really share the founding values of this country, or do they let go of their own to meet the standards in this society?

In search of answers to these questions, and with the support of the Kettering Foundation, I made my way from Dayton to New York, Boston, Louisville, San Francisco, Los Angeles, and Atlanta to interview as many grassroots citizens as I could. I met with people in their community settings, riding Pico Dash and metro lines and even shopping at the 99-Cents Market. I interviewed first- and second-generation immigrants from Korea, China, Holland, Russia, Africa, and Latin America; Muslims from Morocco and Pakistan; American Indians and African Americans. The dialogues covered issues and ideas relating to settlement, life, education, racism, religion, politics (the presidential election), homosexuality, and social value systems (freedom, democracy, and equality). I took extensive notes on my dialogues with the people I interviewed to prevent my own ideas from influencing the findings. I do believe that one's own personal lens could distort the pictures one sees.

The Social-Cultural Model of the "Founding Generation"

Because the term *first generation* is often confusing when referring to foreign-born residents of the United States, I have taken the liberty of defining new immigrants settling in this country as "founding-generation immigrants." Based on my observations, I have come up with the following characteristics that founding-generation immigrants use to describe their settle-transform-sustain process in this country.

1) Settle in this country, start learning the language, and move toward a sense of security by accepting the differences of this society versus their native culture.

2) Observe the social-cultural values and ethics of freedom, democracy, and equality of this country without inserting their own traditional values, being very conscious to abide by the rules, laws, and political correctness in this country.

3) Develop a faith in this country's secularity while still maintaining their own religious beliefs.

4) Transform one's homeostasis from that established in their original motherland to one in which the United States is their official homeland; sustain or guard one's faith and status in this country by becoming part of the social system, raising a family whose original social-cultural traditions are further diluted. (The first-generation born here naturally identify themselves as Americans.)

Almost all the interviewees acknowledged they share the basic and national values of this country: freedom, human rights, democracy, and equality assured by social justice. Only one man from Russia, who has been living in New York City for 17 years, claims to object to the level of freedom in this country.

A Promising Land

Almost all the interviewees acknowledge that they see the United States as a promising place to settle in order to have a better life. They don't see another place that could better fit their interests as immigrants. They believe that the United States is still the strongest and safest country to live in. An East African immigrant who's been living in America for 17 years claims to have realized his American dream: he owns a van for a transportation business and attends a community college after work, where he majors in pharmacology. Grants have helped to subsidize his education and he personally doesn't pay much to attend college. He's got a family in the United States and he says his three-month-old daughter is a godsend. A Chinese cab driver, who has been working in the United States for 10 years, claims his well-being as a Chinese immigrant is highly protected in this country.

Interpersonal Relations and Social Credit

It is strikingly different to me to explore interpersonal relations of "normal" citizens in the United States who are bonded with faith in this shared value system that makes people deal with each other in a more cooperative and civilized way. I have found people to be friendly in the Midwest, even in large cities like New York City and Boston, despite hearing otherwise. I could easily obtain assistance from strangers, with tangible respect. People tend to be trusting and interact in a simple and direct way.

Immigrants I talked to believe they are protected if they follow the rules and laws in this country and keep a sound record. Founding-generation immigrants have repeatedly told me that following the rules in this country is the key point in making their lives successful; they don't see any benefits to breaking the rules. As long as they follow the rules, their equality will be properly protected by the social justice system in this country. These people were also highly aware of self-discipline and financial security. A retired lady in Queens, who came from South Korea in the 1960s, proudly claims that she has a high credit score of nearly 850 points. She believes the key factors for achieving her well-being here in the United States are honesty and diligence.

Political Correctness

I have seen that, in the United States, people in general seem to avoid talking about politics publicly, especially about a presidential election. This is especially true for immigrants. They may see discussion of politics as another issue of political correctness, much like talking about race, homosexuality, religion, and gender issues. They may believe that talking about politics will result in an emotional confrontation with others. During my visits to San Francisco and Boston, I observed people calling for President Obama's impeachment. They even altered Mr. Obama's pictures to resemble Hitler. People were free to take their handouts or not, but I saw no arguments at the scene—an example of freedom of speech and expression that may not exist in some immigrants' countries of origin.

A Conflict of Civilizations?

As a Chinese national, I have only once experienced discrimination in this country when I was called a racist for turning down a solicitation in a market. The worst case of racism I heard of during my interviews was from an African immigrant who has been living in Boston for 20 years. He said someone once told him he should leave this country—that he didn't belong here. He admitted that this hassle happened to him in his early years in Boston, and it was largely due to his language barrier as a new settler. He sees his life in Boston as very positive and he no longer experiences such problems. An American family living in Harlem, whose nationalities are Korean-Chinese and Dutch, find themselves doing really well in their community and have not experienced any discrimination or abuse. Some East African immigrants who have been living in Atlanta for 26 years have told me that they used to face some discrimination issues back in the 1980s, but that it is no longer like that in Atlanta as the residents are becoming more liberal and less conservative. In San Francisco, a Muslim from Morocco told me that he had some hard times shortly after the 9/11 attack occurred, but that his life in the United States is promising because his children are being well educated. A third-generation American Indian descendent told me that, as a cab driver in New York, she could afford to send her daughter to a private high school and her son to college.

In Summary

In my humble observations and findings, I have seen a positive picture of immigrants from all over the world settling in this country, whether to avoid warfare in their native countries or just to start lives here afresh. I have not seen the "clash of civilizations." Rather, the prowess of America is in its people and I believe this country will continue to be a melting pot. I was relieved to find that most of the people I interviewed see China as a trading partner more than a potential threat or enemy, and they believe the Chinese nation to be friendly. A police officer on Wall Street expressed his concerns about China's military buildup; however he believes the common interest between the two countries is big enough to rule out any challenge. (He showed me his gear, badge, and uniform—all made in China, except his 9mm Smith & Wesson pistol.) A female cab driver in New York City discussed China's "One Child" policy with me, while another founding-generation immigrant in San Francisco asked me about China's transition of power and the 18th Party Congress. People largely agree that understanding between the two nations is rare and that we need to increase communication without always listening to the media and "experts."

Endnotes

[1] Francis L. K. Hsu (1909-1999) was professor emeritus of anthropology and a past director of the Center for Cultural Studies in Education at the University of San Francisco. For many years he was chair of the anthropology department at Northwestern University, and in 1977-1978, he served as president of the American Anthropological Association.

[2] "Psychosocial homeostasis" is a research tool developed by Francis L. K. Hsu, which is used to analyze people's relationship to their society through a series of layers: 7th as the Unconscious, 6th the Pre-conscious, 5th the Unexpressed Conscious, 4th the Expressible Conscious as *Jen* (Personage), 3rd the Intimate Society and Culture, 2nd Operative Society and Culture, the 1st layer as Wider Society and Culture, and 0 as the Outer World.

[3] Francis L. K. Hsu, "Psychosocial Homeostasis and Jen: Conceptual Tools for Advancing Psychological Anthropology," *American Anthropologist* 73 (1) (February 1971): 23-44.

Zhang Chunping is director of the International Programs Office at Peking University's School of International Studies (SIS) where he administers three international master's programs and a number of exchange programs with institutions of higher learning in the United States, Korea, and Japan. Zhang is a graduate of SIS in law and international politics.

9

The Rural Issue in Colombia at the National and Local Levels*

by
Angela Navarrete-Cruz

This essay frames the rural issue in Colombia during the administration of President Juan Manuel Santos (2010-2014). Two levels are considered. At the national level, I will identify the discourse related to the issue and how it has evolved in reaction to the mobilization of agricultural workers and ethnic groups. I set out to determine how relevant actors name the problems by analyzing documents and official statements issued by the two primary participants in the debate that has arisen around this issue: the government and the national agricultural workers' movement.

At the local level, in the town of La Mesa, Cundinamarca, I organized a focus group that included diverse socioeconomic stakeholders involved in the issue. The aim of the focus group was to identify how far removed or how close the local actors were to positions defined on the national level.

At both levels my goal was to identify convergences and distinctions between the two on the rural issue, in order to understand and illuminate the complexity of the current debate in Colombia.

---

* This essay is excerpted from a longer report, entitled *Naming and Framing the Rural Issue in Colombia at the National and Local Levels during the First Administration of Juan Manuel Santos (2010-2014)*.

Based on those characterizations, my ultimate goal is to establish an action plan for designing deliberative discussions, which would be sponsored by the Development Foundation for Education, Organic Farming, Agribusiness, and the Environment, known by its Spanish acronym as FUNDEAMBIENTE, to address the rural issue at the local level in La Mesa.

Discourse at the National Level

In order to determine what the discourse at the national level has been for naming and framing the rural issue, I consulted various sources of information, which allowed me to classify the problems and their possible solutions, as well as different points of view with regard to those problems and solutions as presented by the two actors whose positions I studied.

- **From the government:** the 2010-2014 National Development Plan: Prosperity for Everyone[1] (Departamento Nacional de Planeación 2011), the Land and Rural Development Bill[2] (Ministry of Agriculture and Rural Development 2012), and Agrarian Pact[3] documentation.

- **From rural farming organizations:** the Alternative Bill for Agricultural Reform submitted by the National Agricultural Single Trade Union Federation (known in Spanish by its acronym FENSUAGRO) and the National Assembly for Agricultural Unity (2012),[4] as well as the list of demands of the 2013 Catatumbo strikers, the People's National Agricultural Strike, and the mandates for a good life, agrarian structural reform, sovereignty, democracy, and peace through social justice, the basis for the list of demands of the Agrarian Summit: Rural, Ethnic, and Popular, and the Agricultural Strike of April 2014.

This documentation made it possible to identify and classify the issues and their possible solutions based on five concepts: an economic development model put forward by the government, a rural development model, an agricultural development model, agrarian reform, and land policy (understanding that the rural development model includes the last three and agrarian reform includes land policy) (Centro Nacional de Memoria Histórica 2013).

The rural development model refers to the impact of all rural area inhabitants and their social, cultural, political, and economic relationships, including nonagricultural activities. This means that the rural development model is not sectorial and is not exclusively related to economics. That is what differentiates it from the agricultural development model, in which relationship to "economic activities means seeking to increase productivity, increasing income for rural producers" (Pachón Ariza 2011, 49). So the rural development model entails a specific view of the rural world and its relationships to society as a whole.

Rural development is different from agrarian reform because the latter is focused on the structure of landholding and seeks to impact the relationships of economic, social, and political power. In the case of Colombia, land ownership is a source of prestige, as well as political and economic power over a given population (Centro Nacional de Memoria Histórica 2010; 2013).

Finally, land policy addresses territorial organization, land development, and use of soils without necessarily being oriented toward impacting land ownership, although it is related to, and presumably subsumed by agrarian reform (Centro Nacional de Memoria Histórica 2013).

Some of the problems identified in naming the rural issue address, to a greater or lesser degree, these five areas of public policy, and they all differ in definition.

From the National Development Plan to the Joint Agrarian Participation Assembly

The national government pays close attention to, and prioritizes, the agricultural development model in dealing with the country's rural areas. This limited view becomes apparent when we look at matters of general rural development where the population is treated as a production factor. This does not mean in any way that the government is unaware of other specific aspects of public policy but rather that its focus is primarily economic, a limited political and social viewpoint notably lacking in cultural aspects.

This perspective is typical of how development discourse has historically evolved in Colombia, wherein economic factors are deemed essential for the development of society. Hence the importance of measuring the country's productivity for taking public policy action (Restrepo Velasquez 2004). As stated in the National Development Plan (Departamento Nacional de Planeación 2011):

> Economic growth is not a goal in and of itself, but rather a means for achieving well-being and equal opportunities for all members of a society. Economic growth creates jobs, produces wealth and improves quality of life for the population. In addition, economic growth creates public resources that can be used to reduce poverty

and social inequities, or to improve corporate competition (2011, 321). In other words, the theory is that other quality-of-life aspects can be improved by economic growth and so it should be the primary focus of public policy.

In addition, ever since the economic change to the neoliberal model that resulted from the "Washington Consensus," development plans have reflected the need for economic integration with other areas of the world, under the assumption that trade expansion would open the way for economic growth by boosting production in certain areas of comparative advantage over other countries (Guillen 2008). On that basis, Santos' government believes entrepreneurship is what the countryside needs in order to increase productivity and convert those comparative advantages into competitive advantages.

Despite this economics-based perspective of the rural issue, the government has opened up the public agenda in important ways, such as acknowledging that there is armed conflict in the country (the existence of which had been denied by his predecessor, Alvaro Uribe Velez [2002-2010]), and recognizing that there are victims and a need to provide them with material restitution. In this regard, pillars of the 2011 National Development Plan, such as *"equal opportunity"*[5] and *"consolidate peace,"*[6] and the foundational basis of *"good government, citizen participation, and fight against corruption,"*[7] all emphasize the importance of discourse in political and social matters.

Similarly, what stands out is the emphasis on what the government calls development with a territorial focus. This refers to the need for intervention that depends on the differences and particularities in different regions throughout the country. What also stands out is the need to create a network of cities that allow areas of lesser functional capacity to connect with cities that have more (in this case, Bogota, Medellin, and Cali), to promote inter- and intraregional integration that will reduce the gap between urban centers with their "areas of influence." One of the most important tools for achieving this goal, according to the government, are the Areas of Territorial Development (ADT) that are based on geographical division and political-administrative organizations within each of the 32 departments into which Colombia is divided. It is worth noting that according to this focus, there is a profound discursive relationship with what is known as sustainable development, geared toward development models that consider care and responsibility of the environment and the use of natural resources as part of the legacy for future generations (Pachón Ariza 2011).

All of these elements refer to the general development model of society in which, of course, sectorial and specific policies for rural areas are subordinate to what are considered urban areas of influence. Rurality is addressed importantly and specifically as the "driving force of development" in agriculture and rural development. In that regard, there is a recognized need for entrepreneurship in the countryside so the sector can be competitive (according to the logic described above), and in this sense, the rural sector description corresponds to the problems that the agricultural development model needs to address—among these problems, low levels of competitiveness and innovation, scant human capital,[8] inflexible cost structure, insufficient transportation and logistical infrastructure, limitations on market expansion and diversification, and inability to react to external factors and stabilize investment in the countryside. Added to all this is the recognition that it is difficult for the rural population to develop their productive potential because of the persistent armed conflict that plays out primarily in rural areas. In addition, we see that the problem of land concentration contributes to the country's low agricultural productivity.

To the national government, then, it is clear that if the Colombian rural problem is complex, it is essentially related to economics and agricultural activity. Put another way, the government believes that people's living conditions can be improved by strengthening economic growth.

In this regard, it is necessary to point out the fundamental premise of Juan Manuel Santos' government known as "the third route": "the market as much as possible and government as much as necessary." Or, put another way, "the government clears the road, makes the rules, and settles conflict but the private sector and society in general are the ones who build it and use it." This means there is a commitment to reduce government and tremendous confidence that civil society, particularly the market, can take actions aimed at redistribution and economic well-being, the latter being, in the government's view, the basis for improving people's living conditions.

The Land and Rural Development Bill

There is an interesting ambiguity in the proposed solutions to these issues, in that the government's position has changed noticeably as a result of the debate and mobilization of farmers and indigenous and Afrodescendent peoples. This government, whose discourse is conciliatory, unlike that of its predecessor, opened the opportunity for a torrent of collective demands for actions.[9] As a result, the government's position on the rural issue has continued to adjust to include the demands of different social groups, understanding that the Constitutional Court found the rural statute submitted by the Alvaro Uribe Velez administration impossible to execute because no prior consultation with ethnic groups had been conducted (Mondragon 2012).

As noted above, at first the government's proposal had a clearly economic focus, based as it was on the idea that investing resources to strengthen agriculture, forestry, fishing, aquaculture, and production of materials for biofuels could improve conditions in rural Colombia. To that end, the National Development Plan includes seven major proposals to address the bottlenecks and modernize the sector. The Land and Rural Development Bill (Ministry of Agriculture and Rural Development 2012) emphasizes those components even though it should be pointed out that there is tension between a rural development model that responds to the neoliberal (or third-route perspective) in favor of modernizing the countryside through entrepreneurship with a sectorial- and economics-based logic, on the one hand and, on the other hand, a slightly broader point of view that would include basic premises of the human development, focus on matters such as education, health, gender differences, and provide basic public services.

The bill was supposed to be based on the view of rural development seen through a territorial lens that coincides with the general elements identified by the new rurality, but with a significant absence of cultural aspects. Article 2 of the bill defines this focus as:

> [The] process of productive, institutional and social transformation of rural territories in which the local social actors play a leading role and have the support of public, private or civil society agencies, or some combination thereof, for the purpose of improving the well-being of the inhabitants, based on the sustainable use of biodiversity, particularly renewable natural resources and ecosystem services. This process should lead to correcting regional development imbalances (Ministry of Agriculture and Rural Development 2012). To implement this view, the bill proposed decisions that should be made on approaches to rural development programs

Institutional Response to the 2013 Strike: The Agrarian Pact

The bill only envisioned consultation with ethnic communities, as separate from soliciting the opinion of interest groups like mixed-race rural farmers who, together with other social groups, presented a counterproposal for submission in the consultations that MAD held.

Added to that, public protests intensified in 2013 and influenced the slight change in the national government's discursive direction. These events are the foundation underlying what is known as the Agrarian Pact, whereby MAD is conducting a consultation process with stakeholders at the national level, with two goals in mind: constructing a public policy for comprehensive rural development and identifying projects that will improve competitiveness.

To that end, the pact turns again to the CMDRs and CONSEAs, as well as the National Agricultural and Agro-Industrial Council (CNAA) established by Law 301 in 1996. The Regional Councils that operate in five national regions[12] are also included.

The intent of the national government was to use these agencies to create a tiered participatory process in which the 32 departments and 1,105 municipalities in the country would participate. Although CONSEA meetings were planned in all departments, four of them took place after June 3, 2014, which was the deadline for receiving projects. By March of 2014, 641 CMDRs had been created. Of these, 519 were up and running, accounting for 47 percent coverage at the municipal level (Ministry of Agriculture and Rural Development 2014). Activation of the additional 122 CMDRS will bring coverage up to 58 percent.

The pact represents an interesting effort to advance "processes for constructing public policies from the ground up" as characterized by MAD and INCODER, despite being carried out according to MAD's preconceived agenda, omitting discussion of topics like the ZDEs that could conflict with the ZRCs and with other uses of soils. The topics set forth by MAD include diagnostics and a general view of rural development; land and water; productive components; economic, social, and utility infrastructure; and institutions.

According to MAD, the discussions generated should serve as the bases for public policy in the sector and also for the use of approximately one billion pesos' worth of resources for fiscal year 2014. These resources would be distributed through various projects proposed by the CONSEAs and

CMDRs. For rural farmers to be able to access both participation agencies and resources, the government requires them to organize into cooperatives and pre-cooperatives, agricultural and rural companies (including trade groups and associations), or agricultural unions. According to MAD, these requirements promote entrepreneurship processes that are considered to be the first step for achieving higher levels of productivity, and also promote joint work that these types of economic solidarity organizations have the potential to develop (Ministry of Agriculture and Rural Development 2014).

MAD's intention, according to Minister Ruben Dario Lizarralde, is to promote investment in public assets without eliminating subsidies. However, the pact leans toward the "third route," clearly emphasizing trust in the market, as well as the need for neoliberal reforms for managing society. In this regard, not only is entrepreneurship the goal for the rural population so that they can operate in an economy in which free-trade agreements are inevitable, but also so that the rural sector can become more robust and resistant to various risks associated with production in the countryside. This model also aims for partnerships among large, medium, and small producers to create competitive chains and the progressive withdrawal of government. This is also reflected in commercialization activities, where the goal is to strengthen relationships between agricultural workers and large areas for direct marketing, in addition to returning to the idea of collection centers. Nevertheless, the Agrarian Pact includes an incentive for developing rural markets, in contrast to the bill's language, which addresses commercialization only in terms of wholesale commerce, concentrating exclusively on collection centers.

Additionally, there is a strong emphasis on using certified seed that will reduce product variation of crops, such as corn or rice, for which rural farm workers reuse native seed varieties. In this regard, incentives for developing clean, organic agriculture are virtually absent and the green revolution, which has proven to have negative consequences in Colombia, continues to prevail (Vergara 2011).

This view also espouses a return to the EPSAGROs, where technical assistance services would no longer be provided by the UMATAs, which could be completely privatized. Considering the rigid cost structure in this sector, it could be very expensive—and even result in losses—for small and medium producers if they were to take on the responsibility of providing technical assistance. If, on top of that, there is price liberalization for materials—a practice that continues to be promoted because the agricultural model based on the green revolution persists—costs will rise even higher.

The line on land policy is also worth emphasizing. In the first version of the bill, there was significant emphasis on agrarian reform actions based on the idea of agrarian possession, which is diluted in the Agrarian Pact, being reduced to processes for formalizing rural ownership, designating uncultivated land, and returning property within the framework of restitution to victims of the national armed conflict.

The CNAA, as envisioned by the pact, includes limited ethnic and small farmer participation or representation, favoring participation of trade groups (that defend the interests of large-scale producers), despite being the last discussion point that addresses the proposals for a tiered participation process. Indeed, the council should include the participation of various high-level government officials, representatives from among the presidents of the National Federation of Coffee Growers, the Colombian National Entrepreneurs Association (ANDI), the Colombian Farmers Society (SAC), the Colombian Cattle Ranchers Federation (FEDEGAN), and the National Grain Growers Federation (FENALCE). On behalf of farm workers, the pact stipulates participation of a leader from the National Rural Users Association (ANUC), a representative from the black communities, another from the indigenous communities, and another from small rural landowners, all chosen by MAD. In other words, the agricultural workers cannot choose their own representatives (Ministry of Agriculture and Rural Development 2013).

Finally, despite its promises, the Agrarian Pact has missed the mark with regard to radical reform, such as modernizing agricultural conditions in line with rural models that have been developed in other countries where social conditions, as well as natural and public resources, are very different from those in Colombia. In addition, with regard to general development, and specifically in connection with urban/rural relationships, even though there are evident gaps between the two spaces, the desire to impose urban logic on rural living in every aspect is also evident. Without demonstrating any knowledge of rural logic, the pact gives urban needs priority over rural needs so that the city makes no real commitment to the country beyond the processes of commercialization and consumption.

In response to the pact, several rural, indigenous, and Afro-descendant organizations in various departments devised alternative processes, such as the Roundtables of Dialogue and Agreement (MIA), the Agrarian Summit that was held in Bogota in March 2014, and the agricultural strike at the end of April 2014, whereby they expressed their disagreement with the mechanisms for participation established in the pact. According to various leaders, meetings held as prescribed by the pact have been populated by more "suits" than "ponchos," but most important, in discussions on territoriality (a direction the government apparently committed to under the heading of "rural development with territorial focus"), Juan Manuel Santos' government is not willing to commit to that development model, an unwillingness that the rural farmers believe is what keeps them steeped in poverty and beset by various other problems they have to face every day (Sierra 2014). Indeed, the government, as has been noted, views mining as a driving force of development. This has created different conflicts over the environment,[13] soil use, and the government's refusal to recognize the connections that rural, indigenous, and Afro-descendant communities have to the land. Land is vital for rural existence so there is a strong commitment to caring for and preserving the environment, which could be endangered by the government's current mining policy.

So what do rural agricultural workers want? What model do they envision for rural development, agrarian reform, and land policy?

The Demands of Colombia's Rural Population

The rural population has expressed its point of view on what public policy on rural development is and what it should be in at least two different ways. One has been through social protest and a list of demands aimed at the national government. The other way, as noted above, has been by making proposals like the one known popularly as the alternative agrarian reform law, which was drafted in a collective consultation process spearheaded by FENSUAGRO through the National Assembly for Agricultural Unity.

A reading of these documents shows the polarization of the rural debate in Colombia between the national government and the agricultural workers. Their assumptions and perspectives are very different. Here is the text that the rural farmers drafted on the country's current economic model:

> Progress and consolidation of the neoliberal model has done serious harm to the national economy, especially with regard to production, commercialization, and consumption in rural, indigenous, and Afro-descendant communities. This has negatively impacted

food sovereignty for the people and the country. The free market has created a model for dispossession that diminishes quality of life for small producers and works to the benefit of large landholders and multinational agriculture companies. The result has been a blow to the economic interests of rural communities, their cultural practices, and way of life (Cumbre Agraria, Campesina, Étnica y Popular 2014).

The premises for this rural perspective include cultural autonomy, recognition of the rural population as a political player with the right to participate in decisions that impact it directly, and national sovereignty as demonstrated by their defense of food sovereignty, genetic heritage, and local knowledge. These premises are rooted in a development model in which the rural world is viewed as a social space providing concrete, fundamental contributions to all of society. Therefore decent living conditions should be created for its inhabitants, both at the individual and community levels.

This is reflected in the idea for integrated rural development as posited in the alternative bill, where it talks about:

> progressive improvement of the level and quality of life in rural communities, tied to active, organized, and decision-making participation in those communities, in the definition and direction of their development, and in defense of their own interests. Integrated Rural Development requires a transformation of social, economic, and political structures in the rural sector, on the basis of greater equity and social justice, the primary goals of which are: encourage high, sustainable growth in rural production and productivity; raise income in rural communities; and guarantee rural communities' participation in drafting and implementing public policies (FENSUAGRO 2012).

In this regard, the rural population prioritizes development of the rural economy as the basis for building social unity and collective living. Just like the government, the rural population sees tremendous possibility in partnerships based on a shared economy. But while the former believes in a set of partnerships in which companies and large infusions of capital play an important part, the latter envisions partnerships based on a collaborative rural economy led by small and medium producers.

The foregoing is based on logical chaining, recognizing that food is a fundamental right and a social function of people on the earth. If food is a fundamental right, it means public development policies should prioritize food production. In turn, this means that land should be distributed among the highest possible number of owners so that rural farmers, indigenous people, Afro-descendant communities, rural young people, and women can have access to land as a productive resource from which they can build their lives and guarantee food production for national consumption.

This bill provides for the defense and promotion of particular lifestyles in which stewardship of the environment plays a fundamental role, which is a major responsibility of rural communities. In addition, clean, organic production of food for the national market, and the defense of local and ancestral wisdom and knowledge, according to which the use of native seeds should be promoted and protected, are part of the development of a food sovereignty project that would guarantee the right to food for the entire population of Colombia. These points contrast significantly with the government's discourse centered on the use of certified seed (the market for which is monopolized by multinational companies), a bid for radicalizing the green revolution (in clear contrast to organic methods), and trust that market forces will be sufficient for providing food and also for modernizing the countryside.

The government's modernization model recognizes the existence of ethnic groups, but it ignores important aspects of their worldview, such as their knowledge of ancestral methods, like using native seed. Such seed allows for growing and preserving native varieties, which encourages production diversity (Campaña por la dignidad campesina 2012). Certified seed that producers have to acquire in the marketplace, on the other hand, is created in order to minimize product variation, which also creates additional expense for rural farmers. The alternative bill proposes to prohibit the use of genetically modified seed.

The rural population is also in favor of promoting agricultural changes that will allow them to add value to the final product, changes that allow them to form rural agribusinesses that would also generate decent income for vulnerable groups, such as rural women. The bill presented by the national government is silent on this subject. It focuses on diversification of economic pursuits, not on boosting agriculture industry projects or, in this case, small agribusinesses. On the other hand, UMATA technical assistance would still be a service provided by the government to the extent it is deemed essential for developing agricultural activities.

With regard to finances, rural farmers are requesting relaxation of loan terms, production risk insurance provided by the government, and a stop to foreclosures on small rural farms whose owners have defaulted on their debts. The list of demands includes a request for cancelling such debts in special cases (Law 160 of 1994).

On the subject of production, the rural bill recognizes the need to eradicate illegal crops, either manually or through progressive substitution, and advocates for rural decriminalization.[14] A stop to glyphosate spraying has been proposed because, according to rural residents, that substance has been harmful to human health and the environment. The bill also proposes implementing a policy of respect and appreciation of traditional, ancestral uses of coca bushes, poppies, and marijuana in agricultural communities. It is worth noting that the issue of addiction is treated as a health problem, not a criminal problem.

Land development and water districts would be the responsibility of the government, under INCODER, in contrast to the government's proposal to prioritize mixed models for construction and recovery of districts by concessions (awarded to both big industry and rural solidarity-based economic organizations).

Finally, on the subject of commercialization, the rural population proposes eliminating the middleman so that they can sell their products in rural markets, which would allow direct connection between producers and final consumers. This goes along with the need to lower prices for fuel and transportation, and the need to set living wage prices for rural production.

Recognizing the Rural Population as a Political Actor

One of the most important demands of the rural population is to be recognized as a political actor (Salgado 2009), as expressed both in the bill submitted by FENSUAGRO and in the lists of demands presented during the national agriculture strikes of 2013 and 2014.

In response to this request, the government decided to implement the Agrarian Pact process that was not enough for the rural population because public policy decision making is still closed to participation of rural representatives, which became evident with the call to strike issued in April 2014. As a result of that strike, the Joint Agrarian Participation Assembly was created (Ministry of the Interior Decree 870 of 2014, Republic of Colombia 2014) whereby the organizations gathered for the Agrarian, Ethnic, and Popular Summit[15] held on March 15, 16, and 17, 2014, in Bogota to dialogue with representatives of the national government convened by the Ministry of the Interior.

The challenge for the assembly is no less significant. Rural organizations demand spaces to participate in defining both rural public policy and proposals that impact the general development model. As gleaned from their press releases and statements, the rural population maintains a holistic concept of society, and their proposals make evident the need to cooperatively integrate the rights and obligations of urban and rural sectors, in the spirit of reconciliation, integration, and mutual support. In addition, according to the alternative bill for agricultural reform, the aim of rural farmers is to participate in far-reaching decision-making arenas. To that end, they propose institutionalizing decision making from the national to the local levels, under what would be called Integrated Rural Development and Agricultural Reform Councils. At the national level, the rural, ethnic, Afrodescendant, and rural women's organizations would have 80 percent of the decision-making power, and industry trade groups (spokespersons for large businesses and landowners) would not have representation. At the department level it would be 56 percent, and at the municipal level, 77 percent.

They also propose creating a rural National Council for Social and Economic Policy (CONPES) to guarantee articulation of policies on agriculture, production, and rural matters in general, and for resource support for initiatives and decisions made by the councils, with budget approval every February for the following fiscal year.

The alternative bill also includes a proposal for an INCODER board of directors whose decision-making power would be apportioned as follows: 38 percent for the government, 12 percent for national agribusiness union representatives, and 50 percent for rural organizations (including rural women, Afro-descendants, indigenous people, and victims of violence).

The lists of demands are not ignored. In this connection, rural population organizations demand prior consultation with communities that would be affected by land policy, and on every bill that would impact use of soil and their way of life.

Finally, agricultural workers propose institutionalizing participation in every sense, which is much more ambitious than the proposal put forth by the national government. The government's proposal includes various actors, such as educational organizations and other trade groups, of which the rural population is counted as just one more. In contrast, the rural population demands controlling participation, based on the premise that they have been the direct social targets of the national government's relevant policies.

On another front, proposals for appreciating the role played by rural women and the creation of a structure that addresses male discrimination and inequality against women, are much more aggressive and clearly stated in the FENSUAGRO bill. Priority is given to awarding land to rural women, as well as ownership for women separated from their spouses. Other elements, such as recreation and free time, which are absent in the government's proposal, are addressed as rights rather than services in the rural bill.

Finally, it is important to mention the demand for participation in the Havana dialogues between the government and FARC. Rural farmers, ethnic groups, and rural women are recognized as primary victims of the violence perpetrated during the country's internal armed conflict. Thus they demand to be included in the peace negotiations between the government and the FARC guerrilla fighters in order to design an integrated peace policy that would include not only the national dialogue but also regional dialogues in the areas most affected by the conflict.

Territory and ZRCs

ZRCs are seen not only as a mechanism for agrarian reform but also for recognizing social, economic, and cultural rights of the rural population and ethnic groups. For the rural population, any uncultivated land in the country that is suitable for use should be used for these zones, to be created in accordance with Family Agricultural Units (UAF)[16] for mixed-race rural residents and for the indigenous and Afro-descendants, in accordance with their idea of territoriality, with no obligation to link the formation of a ZRC to production projects.

ZRCs represent an efficient self-management system as well as autonomy for rural people that guarantee them the ability to have a life project, as well as adequate use of soil and collective protection of natural resources.

This means pushing aside the ZDE model by prioritizing the needs of the rural population, including displaced persons and victims of violence to whom material restitution will have to be made. According to the government's bill, uncultivated land could be awarded to agribusinesses. In the rural population bill, uncultivated land cannot be so awarded without first meeting the land needs of the identified demographic groups (mixed-race rural farmers, ethnic groups, rural women). In any case, a ZDE award would expire after a maximum of 10 years, and not after 30 years as the government proposes.

This ties in to the subject of national sovereignty. The topic is important to the rural population and is completely ignored in the MAD proposal. It touches on the issues of food and territory, regarding which rural farmers, indigenous people, and Afro-communities advocate for the elimination of surface rights and recovery of national territory from foreign companies to which they would have no access or claim.

In addition, the alternative bill proposes creation of a land fund of administratively expropriated properties of more than 50 hectares that INCODER would manage, based on economic development that must be undertaken for at least three consecutive years.

To summarize, the alternative bill promotes the creation of a strong layer of small and medium landholders at both the individual and collective ownership levels in which economic, social, political, and cultural rights form the foundation for living a good life.

Conclusions

The rural economy is the rural population's foundation for social, political, and cultural development. It also represents a way of preserving their wisdom and ways of life. All these aspects are intrinsically woven together, which is why the rural populations take a position against the view of entrepreneurship held by the national government, which is based on a neoliberal ideology that promotes activities that undermine this type of economy. This is why it has been difficult for the government and the various segments of the rural population to come to an agreement on a public policy for the countryside that would satisfy both actors. This means that the rural mobilizations of 2013 and 2014 cannot be seen as a simple reaction to free-trade agreements. It is an important aspect, but not the only one. What is at stake is an entire way of life in which the economy is a central concern, but not the only one.

The urban-rural perspective of the rural population envisions a number of social rights—health, housing, water, and education—not as a commercially defined set of services, as they are currently treated in this country, but as rights to which the entire population is entitled.

Law 160 of 1994. Republic de Colombia. (August 3, 1994). *Diario oficial [Official Gazette] 41.479.* Bogota. Mesa Nacional Agropecuaria y Popular de Interlocución y Acuerdo Nacional [National and Popular Agricultural Roundtable of Dialogue and Agreement]. (August 2013). *Pliego nacional de peticiones agropecuarias y rurales [National list of agricultural and rural demands]*, Prensa Rural [Rural Press]: www.prensarural.org (accessed April 20, 2014).

Ministry of Agriculture and Rural Development. *Decree 1987 of 2013.* Bogota, 2013.

Ministry of Agriculture and Rural Development (MAD). *ABC del Pacto Agrario.* "Hay campo para todos" [ABCs of the Agrarian Pact. "There is Room in the Country for Everyone"]. Agrarian Pact web site - MAD, www.pactoagrario.minagricultura.gov.co (accessed May 9, 2014).

Ministry of Agriculture and Rural Development. *Pacto Nacional por el Agro y el Desarrollo Rural "Hay campo para todos"* [National Pact for Agro and Rural Development "There is Room in the Country for Everyone"]. Ministry of Agriculture and Rural Development, www.pactoagrario.minagricultura.gov.co (accessed May 27, 2014).

Ministry of Agriculture and Rural Development. *Proyecto de ley de tierras y desarrollo rural (Versión para consulta con pueblos étnicos)* [Land and rural development bill (Version for consultation with ethnic groups]. Bogota, 2012.

Ministry of Agriculture and Rural Development. Instituto Colombiano de Desarrollo rural [Colombian Rural Development Institute]. Camino a una nueva ruralidad [Path Toward a New Rurality]. *El Pacto está en marcha [The Pact is Underway]*, December 2013.

Mondragón, H. "Ley de tierras: un debate que camina" [Land Law: A Debate that Works]. *Revista Semillas* (2012): (46/47), 97-105.

Pachón Ariza, F. *Desarrollo rural: superando al desarrollo agrícola [Rural Development: Overcoming Agricultural Development].* (Bogota: National University of Colombia, 2011).

Restrepo Velásquez, J. "El desarrollo en Colombia: Historia de una hegemonía discursiva." *Revista lasallista de investigacíon,* 1 (1), (2004): 27-36.

Salgado, C. Procesos de desvalorización del campesinado y antidemocracia en el campo colombiano [Processes of Devaluation of the Rural Population and Anti-democracy in the Colombian Countryside]. In *El campesino colombiano [Colombian Rural Farmers]*, by J. Forero, 7-23 (Bogota: Pontificia Universidad Javeriana, 2009).

Sierra, Á. "La movilización es la única salida que nos deja el Estado" *["Mobilization is the only recourse the government leaves us with"]*. March 14, 2014, www.semana.com (accessed May 29, 2014).

Tobasaura Acuña, I. "De campesinos a empresarios: la retórica neoliberal de la política agraria en Colombia" [From Rural Farmers to Entrepreneurs: The Neo-Liberal Rhetoric of Agrarian Policy in Colombia]. *Cuaderno Venezolano de Sociología [Venezuelan Notebook of Sociology]*, 20 (4) (2011): 641- 657.

United Nations Development Program. *National Human Development Report. Rural Colombia. Reasons to Hope.* Bogota: UNDP NHDR, 2011.

Vergara, W. "Desarrollo del subdesarrollo o nueva ruralidad para Colombia. Cartografías del desarrollo rural" [Development of Under development or New Rurality for Colombia. Mapping Rural Development]. *Revista de la Universidad de Lasalle* (55) (2011): 33-58.

Angela Navarette-Cruz is a social analyst in the International Cooperation Office of the Federación Nacional de Cafeteros de Colombia (the Columbian Coffee Growers Association). She has also worked as a project manager for national and local civil society organizations related to the social and education sectors, as a lecturer in political science and as a researcher in democracy, political culture, and rural development in Colombia.

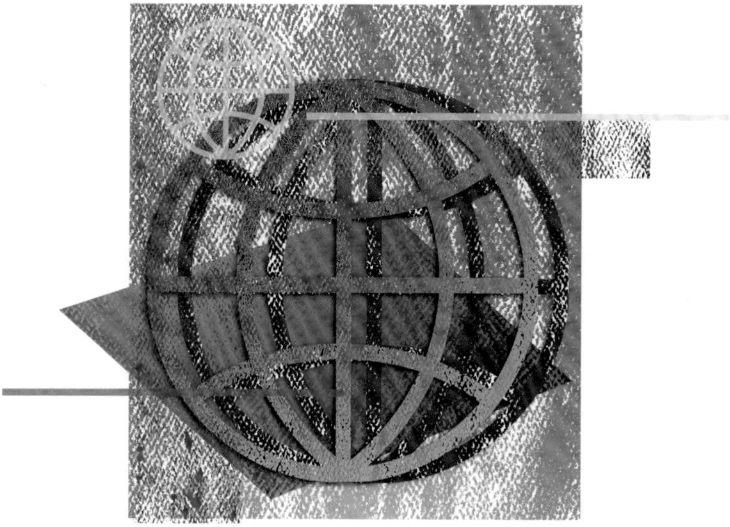

National Identity[1], which soon sparked heated arguments in the United States. Some looked at it as the continuation of the arguments made by Huntington in his book *The Clash of Civilizations*, but the perspective was changed from the world to the United States. Some called it the new 21st-century debate of "racists" and "multiculturalists." Some Americans see Latinos (represented in their minds by Mexican Americans) as a challenge to American culture and its core values, and naturally they turn their attention to this group. Huntington appears to be looking at this from the viewpoint of a so-called "Anglo-Protestant" American, and is worried about the threat to him and his country. But how do those who are the target of his discussion, the "them" he refers to, this group who are outside of "us," define their own status? This question is very interesting and important because, without a doubt, Latino Americans are the real main characters of this story. Looking at the status of "America" or "Americans" from this angle may well reveal a different way of thinking about the issue.

"We" Are Americans, but Not Typical Americans

As is well known, the United States is an immigrant country where one can see people of different colors from all the continents in the world, and Latin America is one of them. In the United States today, one can see signs in both English and Spanish everywhere, and hear conversations in Spanish. And this indicates one reality: this group, which is still called a "minority," has become an important group whose presence can no longer be ignored. According to the US Census Bureau[2], at the end of 2010, the total Hispanic/Latino population of the US was 50,477,594, or 16.3 percent. Among them, the majority are Mexican Americans whose total population is 31,798,258, amounting to 63 percent of the whole Latino/Hispanic population. The next largest is Puerto Rican Americans (4,623,716)[3] and Cuban Americans (1,785,547). The rest—less than a quarter of the total—are from Central America, South America, and regions and countries of the Caribbean. There are not only a large number of Latinos in the United States already, but their numbers will likely increase due to new immigration and higher birth rates. In 2002, the *Economist* magazine published a special report entitled: "Demography and the West: Half a Billion Americans?" which predicted that "as the bulge of Latinos enters peak childbearing age in a decade or two, the Latino share of America's population will soar."[4] Over the past 10 years, at least half of this prediction has been proven true. A recent population census shows that the Latino population increased by 43 percent from 2000 to 2010, which is much higher than the national average (9.7 percent), and it increased from 12.5 percent of the total population to 16.3 percent.[5] That is to say, there is almost one Latino among every six Americans. Another prediction estimates that this ratio will rise to 29 percent by the middle of this century.[6] At that point, nearly one-third of all Americans would be Latinos. These data will certainly raise questions in the minds of many Americans: Will America still be the same country? Will Americans still be the people we now understand as "Americans"? It could well be a looming "identity crisis" in the making.

Since most Latinos in the US are citizens, they are definitely Americans. It seems logical. However, the reality is much more complicated. One of the important reasons why some so-called "true" Americans doubt the status of Latino Americans is because they are newcomers in this immigrant society. In the eyes of some Americans who have long forgotten, or have never traced, their origins, Latinos and their descendants are "immigrants" first, and only second "Americans."

Viewed from the history of several hundred years of immigration, Latinos are indeed latecomers. Following the original "Mayflower" immigration in 1620, America has experienced three large-scale immigration waves. The first wave was from 1840 to 1889. These immigrants were mostly Western and Northern Europeans (chiefly from Germany, Ireland, and England). They represented 82 percent of the total number of 14,269,000 people who immigrated to the United States during this period. The second wave arrived between 1890 and 1919. Although 90 percent of all immigrants were still from Europe, the majority (about three-quarters) were from Southern and Eastern European countries, such as Italy, the Austro-Hungarian Empire, Russia, and Poland. In the third wave—from 1965 to the present[7]—European immigrants were supplanted by immigrants from Latin America and Asia, the great majority from Latin America (see tables on pages 177 and 178).

It is not difficult to see from these charts that Mexican immigrants are the majority among Latin American immigrants. The history of Mexicans immigrating to the United States is relatively long. Large numbers began coming to the United States in the early part of the 20th century, before and after the Mexican Revolution; this wave ebbed with the onset of the

Third Wave of American Immigration (1965–2011)

YEAR AND COUNTRY	NUMBER OF IMMIGRANTS (THOUSANDS)	(%)
1965 to the Present	44,495	100
Latin America	22,111	50
South Asia and East Asia	11,811	27
Europe	5,373	12
Canada	880	2
Africa and Middle East	3,211	7
Other	1,110	2

Source: Pew Research Center Social & Demographic Trends project, *A Portrait of the Adult Children of Immigrants: Second-Generation Americans*, February 7, 2013, 15.

Population of Documented Latin American Immigrants in America Between 1960 and 2010

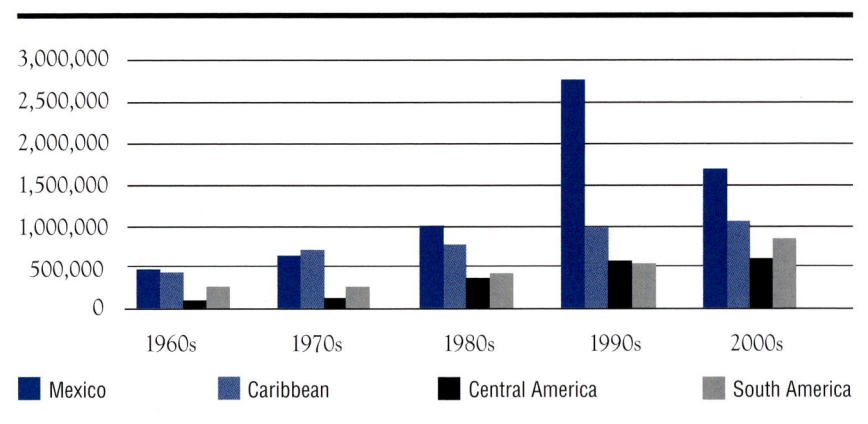

Source: US Department of Homeland Security, *2011 Yearbook of Immigration Statistics*, Washington, DC: DHS, September 2012, 8-10.

Great Depression due to the reduction in the need for labor. During the Second World War, the United States and Mexico signed the Bracero Program Agreement to meet the increased demand for agricultural workers, and many Mexicans came to the United States to do short seasonal work.[8] This program ended in 1964 under the pressure of the human rights move-

Changes in Mexican Immigration to the United States in the 20th Century

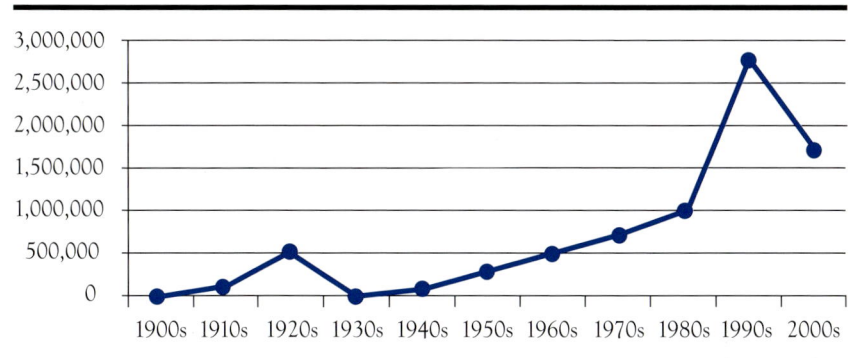

[Chart showing Mexican immigration by decade from 1900s to 2000s, with values ranging from near 0 in early decades, rising to approximately 500,000 in the 1920s, dropping in the 1930s, then steadily increasing to a peak of approximately 2,750,000 in the 1990s, and declining to approximately 1,700,000 in the 2000s. Y-axis scale: 0 to 3,000,000.]

Note: The above data refers to legal immigrants and does not include undocumented immigrants in the same period.
Source: US Department of Homeland Security, *2011 Yearbook of Immigration Statistics*, 8-10.

ment. As noted above, even greater numbers of Mexicans began to flow into the United States after 1965, with the passing of the new immigration law.

Until the 1980s, Cuba had always been the Caribbean country with the most immigrants in the United States. In the 20 years after the Cuban Revolution in 1959, nearly 500,000 Cubans left Cuba for the United States. In the 1980s and thereafter, the Dominican Republic overtook Cuba in the number of immigrants coming to the United States. Immigration from Haiti, Jamaica, and other Caribbean countries also increased rapidly. Most of the immigrants to the United States from Central America are concentrated in a few war-torn countries, such as El Salvador, Guatemala, Nicaragua, and Honduras. In 2011, immigrants from the above four countries accounted for about 90 percent of all immigrants from Central America, with two-thirds of the total from El Salvador and Guatemala. The total number of South American immigrants in the United States prior to the 1980s increased rather slowly, but has increased more significantly since then; since the turn of the century, between 80,000 and 90,000 legal immigrants arrive in the United States every year. Colombia, Peru, and Ecuador are three significant countries from which immigrants come. Immigrants from Brazil have increased in the 21st century; an average of 5,000 a year in the 1990s has recently increased to 12,000 a year.[9]

It is not difficult to imagine from the above data that if we take every 25 years as a generational divide, even the earliest Latin American immigrants (such as the Mexicans who came in around 1910) have experienced four or five generations of changes so far. How could they smoothly shed their immigrant traces to become Americans like other "Americans" within 100 years? To an endless number of new immigrants, it is not surprising that their status as Americans is not recognized. How, then, do these new and old immigrants and their descendants define their status? According to the report on Latinos in America issued by the Pew Research Center in 2012, when asked to describe their own status under most circumstances, only 20 percent think of themselves as "American." About half of them carefully expressed that although they are American citizens, they are conscious of the fact that they are "hyphenated Americans"; or in their own words: "very different from typical Americans."[10]

Who are the so-called "typical" Americans? Obviously, this question has more than one answer. However, what is unspoken is obvious. That is, there exists a certain invisible dividing line among Americans; on one side of it are typical Americans, and on the other side are—let us temporarily call them "atypical" Americans. I asked the same question to "typical" and "atypical" Americans—based on my assumption—I met. When Paloma Dallas, who was my colleague when I worked at the Kettering Foundation, first heard this question, she was kind of startled. After considering it for a while, she replied that this was a difficult question to answer because of the diversity of the country and particularly because of its history of difficult race relations.[11] Victor García, a Mexican American friend of Dallas, was born in a suburb of Mexico City and immigrated to Minnesota with his father in 1962. He is now the president of the nonprofit social organization Del Pueblo, Inc., which particularly serves Latino communities. In his view, the invisible dividing line between typical and atypical Americans is not only based on visible differences, such as color of skin and language, but also on elements that can be felt but are not verbalized (such as culture), which exert an even more important influence. Using his personal experience as an example, he has discovered that in his daily life he not only shares the same language with other Latinos, he can also communicate better with the majority of Americans from Asian cultures. By way of comparison, he felt more isolated from both white Americans and African Americans. Moreover, he feels that social status is another, even more complicated, element.[12] Frank Bergmann, who is the owner of an architecture company in Wisconsin and who has hired dozens of Mexican Americans, agreed with this view to a certain degree. He said that although he is a white American, he is not a typical American. From his point of view, the latter refers to the urban rich class. He himself grew up on a farm; even though he moved to a city and owns properties, he does not feel that he belongs to this group.[13] The answer offered by Kenneth Pomeranz of the Department of History at the University of Chicago is more "academic." He believes that typical Americans can refer to those in a specific time period (especially from the end of the Second World War to the 1970s) who "believed they naturally possessed the happy life." Whether or not they went to college, it was not hard for them to obtain a steady lifelong job. Even for the blue-collar class, one person's income was completely sufficient to support a whole family and lead a comfortable life. That period of time has passed, but this complexity still exists.[14] We can see from these few answers that no matter how we define the concept of typical American, Latinos are excluded. Then, who are they?

Hispanic? Latino? Or . . . ?

As atypical Americans, Latinos are generally called *Hispanic* or *Latino*. These two technical terms, respectively, began to be used in the 1970s and the 1990s. On June 16, 1976, the US Congress passed the "Joint Resolution Relating to the Publication of Economic and Social Statistics for Americans of Spanish Origin or Descent," which is Public Law No. 94-311.[15] In May of the next year, the word *Hispanic* was first used in a directive issued by the US Office of Management and Budget (OMB) to standardize the collection and reporting of racial and ethnic statistics. Twenty years later, the OMB revised this order and added the term *Latino* as a synonym to *Hispanic*, and they were used interchangeably.[16] Both terms have been used to indicate Latin American immigrants and their descendants up to the present day.[17]

In reality, there is a distinction between these two terms. The term *Hispanic* came from *Hispaicus*, which, in turn, came from *Hispania* (that is, *España*). Strictly speaking, it refers to those who speak Spanish in Latin America. There are 18 countries in Latin America where the official language is Spanish: Mexico, Guatemala, Costa Rica, Honduras, Nicaragua, El Salvador, Panama, the Dominican Republic, Cuba, Colombia, Venezuela,

Ecuador, Peru, Bolivia, Chile, Argentina, Paraguay, and Uruguay. The residents of Puerto Rico, a territory under the jurisdiction of the United States, also mostly speak Spanish.

Latino, on the other hand, covers *all* Latin American groups, not just those who speak Spanish. *Latino* also includes immigrants and their descendants from Portuguese-speaking Brazil and other English-speaking countries and areas (Trinidad and Tobago, Jamaica, the Bahamas, Antigua and Barbuda, the Barbados, Guiana, Belize, Saint Lucia, Saint Vincent and the Grenadines, Grenada, Dominica, the Federation of Saint Kitts and Nevis, the Bermuda Islands, Cayman Islands, Montserrat Islands, Turks and Caicos Islands, the American Virgin Islands, the British Virgin Islands, and Anguilla); the French-speaking countries and areas (Haiti, French Guyana, Martinique, and Guadalupe); and the Dutch-speaking countries and areas (Surinam, Dutch Andes, and Aruba).

However, as noted, officially no such distinction is made. According to the *Revisions to the Standards for the Classification of Federal Data on Race and Ethnicity*[18] issued in October 1997 by the US government, race and ethnicity (Hispanic/Latino) are two different concepts. Starting in the same year, the OMB asked the federal government organizations to use at least five racial classifications: white, black or African, Asian, American Indian or indigenous Alaskan, and native Hawaiian or resident of the Pacific Islands. For those who could not be classified into the above classifications, the Census Bureau introduced a sixth classification in 2000: "some other race." However, Hispanic or Latino is not included in this. The explanation in the census form says that Hispanic or Latino means those who are from Cuba, Mexico, Puerto Rico, Central and South America, or another Spanish-speaking culture or ancestral home. Based on this, those who identify themselves as Hispanic or Latino can be of any race. As to who belongs to this group and who does not, at present, the official data is based on self-identification of those who are surveyed. In other words, whether an American is classified into this group all depends on how he or she fills out the official survey data.

Do Latin American immigrants and their descendants identify with these two labels? What can be said for certain is that immigrants and their descendants, other than those from Latin America, generally will not, and probably cannot, identify themselves as belonging to this category. They will select from the five racial categories or say that they belong to "some other race." In fact Hispanic and Latino people do not really identify with such so-called "Pan-ethnic" labels. But when filling in national census questionnaires and faced with these two labels, and knowing they will be viewed by others as belonging to one of those groups (Hispanic or Latino), it is difficult for them not to choose one of these labels. Some Latinos may turn to the race section and select one according to skin color: immigrants and their descendants from countries like Haiti, Cuba, or Dominica, where black or mixed ethnicity is more prevalent will choose "black or African American"; those who are from such countries as Argentina, Uruguay, Costa Rica, Chile, or Brazil where at least half of the population is white, may choose "white"; and Chinese Americans or Japanese Americans from Peru, Cuba, or Brazil may choose "Asian." However, the majority of those who are from places where Indian-European mixed-ethnicity individuals are in the majority and under the circumstance where there is no Mestizo or other related race to choose from, "Hispanic" or "Latino" are the only (or at least the first) label they can identify with.[19] As can be imagined, the statistical results from this method of data collection can be very fuzzy and it is very difficult to know the exact self-identification of each Latin American group. In fact, such methods as sampling and interviews give a much clearer picture than the data collection conducted by the Census Bureau. The Latin American Research Program of the Pew Research Center took an opinion poll of 1220 randomly selected Latino adults between November and December 2011 in the 50 states and Washington, DC. Their findings showed that only a quarter of them felt inclined to label themselves as "Hispanic" or "Latino." Among them, the second- and third- or later-generation adults preferred "Hispanic" to "Latino," because they believed that the latter sounded too much like a "minority race" and too much like "a term used for foreigners." However, their fathers' or grandfathers' generations (including the first generation and a small number of second-generation adults) and the newly arrived Latin American immigrants preferred to call themselves "Latino." This is because they have a closer (and unseverable) relationship with Latin America than they do with the United States, or *El Norte* as they called it. And "Latino" reflects common language, religion, heritage, and even blood ties that not only give Latin Americans with is very strong and no matter how different their original culture is from American culture. There may be a difference in their paths, methods, and characteristics of the stages of assimilation, but largely they do not have the choice of "not being assimilated," as decidedly put by Huntington.[29]

The "direct line" assimilation process of traditional theory and the "racialized" assimilation process, both often discussed, are all realized among Latinos, especially their descendants.[30] Generational changes, the influence of English, the rise in educational level and upward mobility, changes in residential environment, interracial marriages, identity consciousness connected to racial status, and other elements all push changes in Latino assimilation and identity. Owing to the spatial limitations of this paper, only the first two aspects will be discussed in greater detail below.

The differences in the identity of different generations is clearly reflected in the research data. At present, among Latinos of all ages, the number of second-, third-, and later-generations born in the United States now far exceeds the number of first-generation immigrants born in other countries. The ratio is respectively 63 percent and 37 percent.[31] Just like other immigrant groups, as generations extend, later generations of Latino families similarly exhibit ever more obvious characteristics of Americanization (and at the same time, a certain degree of "de-Latin Americanization"). Owing to the fact that they have not had the experience of living there, their ideas about their ancestral countries is more of an abstract concept. They may admit to their ancestral roots, but this does not mean that they identify with their countries of origin or the cultures and ethnic systems. Simply put, acknowledging their ancestry and identifying themselves by it are two different issues.

Language, like identity, also changes with the extension of generations. The language of the host society plays a very important role in the assimilation process. Furthermore, English or "the English cultural heritage," according to Huntington, is at the core of "American characteristics."[32] From the related data available at present, one cannot see whether there is any difference between Latinos and other immigrants (for example, Asians) born in the United States. Although many people can use Spanish to varying degrees because of a bilingual education, English is doubtless their first language (see the charts above). At the same time, many first-generation immigrants and newly arrived immigrants still mostly use Spanish as their main language. When I interviewed Pablo Piccato, a Mexican American at the Institute of Latin American Studies (ILAS) of Columbia University, he emphasized the fact that for those people who do not speak English, it is not because they are "unwilling" or "do not want to" or purposely reject English; rather, it is because they "cannot" speak English. In fact, they are aware that in order to get a good job and improve their living conditions, they "must speak English." And the reason that they "cannot" is largely because they lack language training and the ways and means of acquiring a "good education."[33]

As noted above, in addition to the factors of generation and language system, mobility owing to a rise in educational level and other elements will make the corresponding groups and their descendants change their identities unconsciously—or consciously, which implies deliberately distancing themselves from Latin American identity and culture. Correspondingly, marriage with other racial descendants and racial groups also makes their descendants feel ambiguous about their Latin American identity.[34] When only one parent is of Latin American descent, or is of mixed Latin American heritage, the possibility of the children identifying themselves as Latin American is small. Under such conditions, it is easiest to change racial status. In other words, the children or descendants of these families will have a greater likelihood of choosing a more definitive racial identity, such

English Proficiency of Different Generations of Latino Americans and Asian Americans

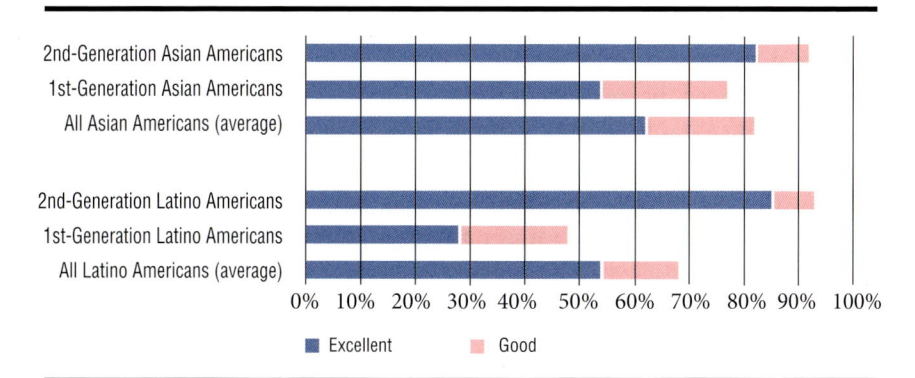

Source: Pew Research Center, "A Portrait of the Adult Children of Immigrants: Second-Generation Americans," February 7, 2013, 49.

[9] For related data, refer to US Department of Homeland Security, *2011 Yearbook of Immigration Statistics*, 8-10.

[10] Pew Research Center, *When Labels Don't Fit: Hispanics and Their Views of Identity* (Washington DC, 2012), 10.

[11] Interview with Paloma Dallas, Dayton, Ohio, April 20, 2013.

[12] Interview with Victor Garcia, Centerville, Ohio, May 2, 2013.

[13] Interview with Frank Bergmann, Cancun, Mexico, May 11, 2013.

[14] Interview with Kenneth Pomeranz, Chicago, May 1, 2013.

[15] For details, refer to *Joint Resolution Relating to the Publication of Economic and Social Statistics for Americans of Spanish Origin or Descent (Public Law 94-311)*, June 16, 1976, http://www.gpo.gov/fdsys/pkg/STATUTE-90/pdf/STATUTE-90-Pg688.pdf.

[16] For a related directive and revised document, refer to: *Directive No.15 Race and Ethnic Standards for Federal Statistics and Administrative Reporting*, May 12, 1977. http://wonder.cdc.gov/wonder/help/populations/bridged-race/directive15.html; *Revisions to the Standards for the Classification of Federal Data on Race and Ethnicity*, October 30, 1997, http://www.whitehouse.gov/omb/fedreg_1997standards.

[17] For the birth and background of these two concepts, refer to Rubén G. Rumbaut, "The Making of a People," in *Hispanics and the Future of America*, edited by Marta Tienda and Faith Mitchell, 16-65 (Washington, DC: The National Academic Press, 2006).

[18] For details, refer to http://www.whitehouse.gov/omb/fedreg_1997standards.

[19] In recent years, some individuals or organizations who promote Latino rights enthusiastically call for Mestizo/Mestiza to be incorporated into present population census data as a selection for race. There are many opinions for and against this idea. Refer to: Marissa Mitchell, "Shaping Identities: Young Hispanics Don't Fit into Distinct Categories," http://northwestern.news21.com/identity/shaping-identities-young-hispanics-dont-fit-into-neat-categories/#storytop.

[20] Pew Research Center, *When Labels Don't Fit: Hispanics and Their Views of Identity*, 6-14.

[21] Edward Retta and Cynthia Brink, "Latino or Hispanic Panic: Which Term Should We Use?" http://www.crossculturecommunications.com/latino-hispanic.pdf.

[22] Pew Research Center, *When Labels Don't Fit: Hispanics and Their Views of Identity*, 12-13.

[23] Refer to: Danny Quintana, *Caught in the Middle: Stories of Hispanic Migration* (Silver Spring, MD: Beckham Publications Group, Inc., 2012), 258.

[24] Interview with Victor Garcia, Centerville, Ohio, May 2, 2013.

[25] Portuguese, which is the second largest language in Latin America and the official

language of Brazil, is of the same root with Spanish and is rather close to it. The speakers of either language can communicate with speakers of the other one.

[26] Pew Research Center, *When Labels Don't Fit: Hispanics and Their Views of Identity*, 23, 25.

[27] Under most circumstances, these two concepts express similar or duplicate implications according to Milton Gordon, meaning the result of the "meeting" of different races or nationalities. Sociologists often use *assimilation,* while anthropologists often use *acculturation*. Refer to Milton M. Gordon, *Assimilation in American Life: The Role of Race, Religion and National Origins* (New York: Oxford University Press, 1964), 61.

[28] Gordon, *Assimilation in American Life*, 80, 88.

[29] Huntington, *Who Are We?* 149-152, 181-182.

[30] As for the discussion of assimilation relating to "racialization," refer to: Tanya Golash-Boza and William Darity Jr., "Latino Racial Choices: The Effects of Skin Colour and Discrimination on Latinos' and Latinas' Racial Self-Identifications," *Ethnic and Racial Studies*, 31, no. 5 (2008): 899-934.

[31] Pew Research Center, *When Labels Don't Fit: Hispanics and Their Views of Identity*, 11.

[32] Huntington, *Who Are We?,* 178.

[33] Interview with Pablo Piccato, New York City, March 29, 2013.

[34] According to more recent data, compared to white, black, Asian, or other groups in American society, the second, third, and later generations of Latin Americans born in the United States have a much higher ratio of marriage to other races, 26 percent and 31 percent respectively. Refer to Pew Research Center Social & Demographic Trends project, *Second-Generation Americans: A Portrait of the Adult Children of Immigrants*, 6.

[35] For related discussions, refer to Amon Emeka and Jody Agius Vallejo, "Non-Hispanic with Latin American Ancestry: Assimilation, Race, and Identity among Latino American Descendants in the US," *Social Science Research*, 40 (2011): 1547-1563.

[36] Even though Latin American immigrants (especially new immigrants) in the last 20 some years show the tendency of dispersing to different states, most of them still concentrate in the western and southern parts of the country. States with higher ratios of Latino populations include: New Mexico (46.3%), California (37.6%), Texas (37.6%), Arizona (29.6%), Nevada (26.5%), Florida (22.5%), and Colorado (20.7%). Refer to Sharon R. Ennis, et al., *The Hispanic Population: 2010* 2010 Census Briefs, (US Census Bureau, May 2011), 6.

[37] Near my rented apartment when I was with the Kettering Foundation, there is the Dayton International School, which specializes in teaching Spanish. Somewhat surprising is the fact that the main target is not the imagined Latino American children but the "American" children born in non-Spanish speaking families. The intention of the school, as stated on its website, is quite interesting: "The Dayton International School (DIS) prepares students

with the academic, social and language skills needed to be successful in our multicultural, multilingual world. DIS provides a bilingual education that fosters intercultural understanding and a global perspective," http://www.daytonis.org/mission.html.

Guo Jie is an associate professor at the School of International Studies (SIS) at Peking University, where her teaching and research responsibilities focus chiefly on Latin America and Central and Eastern Europe. Guo, who earned a PhD at SIS, is the author of numerous articles and three books: The 1956 Hungarian Revolution: US Policy Responses, Nagy and Hungary in the 1950s, *and* Declassified American Intelligence Archives on China.

11

An Interview with Maureen Gillon

by
Maura Casey

Q. *Perhaps we could start with a description of your history with the Kettering Foundation. I know you were an international fellow in 2013, but your involvement goes back further.*

A. That's right. My initial contact with the Kettering Foundation was in 1999. I was a Porirua city councilor (elected member of local government) then, and I was nominated to attend a workshop in Wellington, New Zealand, run by associates of the foundation. About 30 of us spent a full on week working together, to learn about Kettering's approach to the practice of deliberative democracy as a starting point for community action. This was in stark contrast to the consultative model that we were using in the community and in local government. This was the starting point of learning from experience and it highlighted how useful it could be and what a different quality of information could be gained. This was the beginning of a new era of "talking" in the Porirua community and provided a way for community voices to have a say, rather than hearing just from the organizations. This also began a period of deliberative practice that made it possible for diverse views to contribute to local discussion and decision making.

A couple of years later I was invited to the Kettering Foundation to attend a workshop called the Deliberative Democracy Workshop (DDW), and then again the following year for another DDW workshop. With each stage of the journey I learned more about the value of deliberative practice, and understanding more about the philosophy made a difference. Moving beyond the methodology of deliberation to understanding more about the "movement," provided a touchstone, and a better basis for exploring what and why we were engaged in this work. It was not just a series of facilitated workshops but a local movement where like-minded people were beginning to form around new ideas and practices by sharing experiences and ideas. Over time, this critical mass of people has become a powerful element; it's been an evolutionary approach to growth and change. Occasionally touching base with Kettering has been of enormous value to me and others who have been fortunate to be invited. This has resulted in consolidating knowledge and practice as people have found spaces in the community to meet and talk, formally and informally. The ability to test ideas and share experiences has enabled people to grow in confidence as they contribute and see their ideas come to fruition. This work has increased the level of participation in the city. There are now more opportunities as people discover the use of deliberation for moving on their issues. Informality is essential, although there are times when people need to move an issue forward and this means moving into a more formal space to deliberate on a larger scale.

For the core group, it has been encouraging to see the growing expertise in deliberative practice. The growing network of like-minded people has resulted in an increased ability to move issues forward, and as their confidence has grown, they have moved into their own communities to practice. Our processes have matured over time as we've learned from our own experience.

Q. *How have you applied what you've learned about deliberation into your community work?*

A. Initially, I worked with those who had been at the Kettering workshop in Wellington. We agreed to work together to harness action to address health disparities affecting people in our community. We prepared to hold a deliberative forum. Matters to address before the forum were community relationships and community mandate. Community leaders, including the mayor, agreed to participate and provided public acknowledgement of the initiative. This provided the credibility needed for agency participation. Those invited were community leaders and stakeholders responsible for decision making, funding, and service delivery. Two hundred community and agency leaders attended the forum. We used deliberative practice to identify how we would work together on matters of concern. We also identified a core group of about 20 people to continue to work on community solutions. We encountered a few problems with the process due to inexperience, and found that if the process is compromised then you don't achieve the depth or quality of information that you need to move forward. And when you shorten the process, you can lose traction, which may be hard to regain.

Following the forum, a leadership group pursued agreed-upon actions. The goal was to establish Porirua as a Center of Excellence in health-care delivery, which began with a learning journey to understand how different groups could work together to reduce disparities in health through participation in collaborative action.

Q. *Can you give me an example of the different groups involved?*

A. The diverse group of community leaders and local decision makers included representatives from the Ministry of Health and the chair of the District Health Board, which provides planning and funding of health services for the entire region; he was interested because of the disparities in health-care delivery, increasingly poor health outcomes in Porirua, and significantly increased costs of health care. Participants also included local clinical leaders from community and hospital services, representatives from Maori and Pacific communities, local academic institutions, and the City Council. Our focus was on how a local health system could work collaboratively to address an area of disparity. To help focus everyone's attention, clinical leaders identified the main concern as an increase in diabetes. The Ministry of Health officials offered to identify known benchmarks for health in the area to identify the incidence of diabetes. Local clinicians and others described their experiences and perspectives. The local council identified its role as a repository of information and recorded activity. (This put activity and contributions in the public domain and enabled us to grow the evidence base and use information for negotiating new services or additional funding for access to those services). The council identified service and funding opportunities and also worked with the community and with Ministry of Health officials to identify access and measures for monitoring change. Community leaders, local supermarkets, and health services worked together on a healthy-eating-healthy-action (HEHA) approach to help people learn about healthy food, and ran food tours. And the sport and recreation area of the council worked with local health services, while communities began planning walking activity around the city. Collaboration formed around joint activity in a "competitive and crowded" space. It resulted in new relationships forming as people and organizations began to connect and work together.

Holding regular meetings using deliberative practice enabled people to listen to different perspectives, explore options, understand tensions or conflict, and test new ideas in a safe forum. The experience of working together in this way resulted in the formation of relationships and the emergence of collaborative activities. This enabled the Center of Excellence forum to take a step back as activity began to be integrated in the diverse organizations involved and people began to find their places in the process.

Q. *So the process made the need for more such forums—at least on health issues—less necessary?*

A. That was right for a time. The local system began to take on a life of its own and the experience of being involved in the process over a long period had given people and organizations confidence to try their own ideas. We saw community action on diabetes go to a whole new level as communities and families developed their own ideas about "getting active." Schools also identified how healthy eating and healthy action could be integrated into their curricula. Churches and community organizations were running HEHA classes with a focus on preventing diabetes. Together, the Ministry of Health, City Council, and District Health Board had identified measures and were monitoring the impact of local activity. The problem is that early momentum was lost because the dialogue did not continue in a public place and activities were institutionalized. Continued sustainability seems to demand a place for people to connect with others through storytelling.

Those actually in the process had become quite active at local and government levels, with the level of communication and information sharing increasing as lessons from the experience were linked with improvement. Continued inclusion of community decreased with the demise of the local health forum.

Q. *So, after this process of engagement concerning diabetes, did you pick other health issues to work on?*

A. Yes, the ministry had worked with the city to produce a report ("The Porirua Health & Disability Plan" can be accessed on the Internet). Some of the lessons from that report were adapted or translated by others in the New Zealand health system, and the plan underlays the continuing work by community, health providers, and other organizations. It was around this time that I went back to the Kettering Foundation and participated in the DDW workshops, and I came back quite fired up, particularly about how to actually connect people in the process. During this same time period the Porirua City Council had commissioned research about citizen satisfaction with council services. The report identified "low-value" and "high-value" citizens and recommended that city funding should be targeted at high-value citizens. I don't know if you've ever come across that before, but this approach discriminates against the most powerless people in society and rewards the most powerful, creating even more disparity.

Q. *Who were among the low-value citizens and who were among the high-value?*

A. The report described high-value citizens as those living in the more well-off villages who were paying tax rates on high-value properties. They had higher incomes and the perception was that this group added more value to the local economy because of its earning power than did low-income (low-value) citizens. Those living in government housing were not considered to be high-value residents because they paid rent, and there was a perception that they did not add value to the local economy because they did not pay taxes. In fact this is not correct, as taxes are accounted for in the amount paid to landlords. People living in these areas are the most economically disadvantaged and do not have the same level of access to resources as those in other parts of the city. Many people were shocked by the description and community concern over the concept of "low-value" citizens was a catalyst for community action.

The city of Porirua is geographically defined by eight quite separate villages with a wide range of incomes. The council report that described people with low incomes as "low-value residents" did not mention any role for them in the life of the city.

This spurred an extensive and ongoing community discussion that resulted in community action to get the council to value *people* rather than what they earned. The result was that this altered concept was embedded into all the formal city structures, which enabled funding to be directed to activities that supported all the people in the city.

Community action resulted in people having more say in civic affairs, the environment, facilities available to people, and how they participate in city life. The approach was described in an application for an international award Porirua won—the Livable Community award in Chicago in 2010. It's on the Porirua City Council website. [*From the website: "Porirua City topped the Community Participation and Empowerment criteria when judged against all other 43 cities entered, regardless of population size, including cities such as Norwich, England, Miami Beach, Fla. and Wuxi (China)."*]

As part of the approach, people were invited to identify their own village plan. When they decide they want to put together a plan they approach the council with their concept. The council encourages them to implement it and so each of those villages has now really taken on a life of its own.

And so now the council participates in activities arranged so that they are working together. And I can tell you that the environment and the atmosphere in those communities have changed a lot. People are now taking more pride in their communities and they are becoming more actively engaged.

I think it came about purely around relationships and connecting in the beginning, and then people began to meet and talk about their ideas.

Of course, a lot of those villages were not keen to participate in the beginning.

There were one or two villages that were early adopters with everyone else watching. When the others saw what was happening and that it was driven by the community rather than by the council, they were in. The delight for me was when I saw that a village that had been the most negative came forward and became engaged. They had seen the value for themselves. One of the things about the approach is that people have to consider themselves not only in their own village, but how they contribute to the life of Porirua City as a whole.

So it's been a very exciting thing to be part of. Our current mayor, Nick Leggett, is now going to take it a step further and he's got this whole idea of how you get kids involved and how you get schools working more closely with communities and so that's a whole new adventure for them. And he's generated huge excitement around that.

Q. *It sounds like you got great results. Tell me how many years this took. Do you have any "before and after" results—any example you can give of what took place? How many years did this process take? You started a number of years ago did you not?*

A. We started in 1999. These things take time.

Q. *The process took 10 to 15 years?*

A. Yes, and we are still learning. But now, the community has many more mechanisms for talking if they want to get an issue on the table. People have ways of working in the communities that may not have been there before. People now feel like they've got mechanisms to change things if they want to.

In fact I'd say that city connectedness is very, very high and that's something that's been enabled by young people and technology as well.

Q. *So you're a veteran of deliberation now.*

A. I could say I was a veteran, but I am very much a learner I would say.

Q. *Did you have any statistics on how deliberation had an impact on community health?*

A. We do actually. "The Porirua Health and Disability Plan" can be accessed on the Internet. It's got a written statement of action on health.

Q. *So, after the issue of diabetes did you tackle others, such as high blood pressure or high cholesterol?*

A. Personally I didn't, but all the related parties who were actually working in those areas began to use the processes to tackle these issues. The most recent that I can think of is addressing rheumatic fever. That's actually quite a neat, tidy issue, because you can see a start and a finish very quickly.

Q. *You saw a more immediate result there?*

A. Yes. You can check the website to see the Porirua Rheumatic Fever project. Another area that we're working in is connecting communities and education to raise educational achievements. There's currently a randomized control trial going on the subject of helping children improve their ability to read. It is called the Shine Literacy project, and it's on the ShinePorirua website.

Q. *Shine is one of the organizations that you direct, is that correct?*

A. I am the cochair of the Shine Porirua Education Initiative. It's really a movement around raising achievement for children in Porirua. Shine is a collaboration of people with resources, knowledge, or experience, who want to work with others to raise achievement in education. So, again, it's one of these things that's not centered in an organization, but rather revolves around mutually reinforcing activities and collaboration across the system. The structure and work of the Shine Porirua Education Initiative is modeled on the Strive Partnership of Cincinnati, a group of leaders from various sectors who came together in 2006 with the goal of improving academic success in the urban core of that city.

The literacy project is one of our key activities. It began with an educator who discovered that not all children benefited from the current literacy curriculum and identified patterns that might provide barriers to learning. She tried a new method and produced a 30 percent increase in literacy in the test school. Now they're teaching the educators how to teach a new component of literacy and it's the subject of a randomized control trial, which is using the methodology developed by Joy Allock (whose published paper is on the Shine website).

Q. *At what grade level does this intervention take place?*

A. Year four. The outcome of this will be that education policy, planning, funding, and the curriculum will need to change, that teacher training will need to change, and continuing professional development will also be implicated. Government buy-in and funding will need to drive changes. So we are working in all areas that will be impacted by this change.

This work involves working with children, families, and communities as well so it's quite a broad piece of work that covers all the 34 primary schools in our area and some outside schools that were included in the randomized trial.

Q. *Was there a deliberative process involved to begin this?*

A. No, this began in the usual way with educators and communities saying let's work on this and teachers saying we're doing the best we possibly can. We can't do this on our own. We're beating our heads against a brick wall. Help.

And so through the networks there were a couple of meetings that I was asked to chair. The upshot of that was nearly a year of discussions with community leaders, educators, principals, Ministry of Education, local government, boards of trustees (parents), and key community organizations. We developed measures and planned for an Education Summit in a full deliberative forum attended by about 200 people.

Participants in that forum identified a number of areas to be addressed, including literacy, digital enablement (access to technology and learning how to use it), and youth transition (from secondary school to further education and employment).

Another forum was organized around a concept called Schools in the City, which is a citywide integrated education system connecting preschool, primary school, secondary school, and tertiary institutions, such as private training establishments, universities, and workplace training, in the city in a seamless approach to helping children learn. And that also brings in the boards of trustees, which are made up of parents.

Q. *You've been involved in seeing deliberation work in your community in two very different realms, in health and in education.*

A. When I went to Kettering, it was to look at our process. We were struggling with the extent of the collaboration. I had a whole lot of things that were just jumbled in my mind. I think if I hadn't gone to Kettering to do that work at that point it would have been a disaster, because it was getting very, very complicated. Having that time to think and learn really helped. I produced an evaluation methodology, and because I'm working in the process as well as writing, this all is taking time, but the learning and the way it's informing the process has been amazing. We are all learning from the experience.

I'm working with a team of people and we use the learning from that to inform every part of the process. We always go back to the deliberative process to ask questions like "what are we missing here?"

Q. *Can you imagine other subjects that you'd like to use deliberation in but haven't quite had time?*

A. In my experience these topics have always come to us through the networks and people raising concerns and/or wanting to get involved in some way.

This education initiative is going to be a very long-term activity, but you can actually see some real progress with some of the activities.

All of the external data said our city had a problem. We had no local data but we knew we had very poor results in all the colleges.

Also, as we have entered into this process the importance of knowing the sources of information has become clear, particularly as some information was not shared. Now that there is a set of measures about local education, developed by working group participants, it has been possible to build connections with organizations that hold data. All have agreed to share data and the local council has agreed to collect, manage, and report it. We can now share information across our education system and use it to negotiate with government departments about education opportunities or needs in the city. For the first time we have a set of measures about the children's learning continuum in the city, which we have never had before.

Q. *So data is informing your deliberation.*

A. It has to, although we also need community information to enable us to understand the context of the data. In the health project, we did not have a local benchmark for health data so we had no lever to negotiate. You can talk about different ways of working, but you need that baseline. Before the health project in 2000, there had been one needs assessment completed 20 years before, but it produced insufficient information to guide change. Now information is produced on a yearly basis to inform planning. With regular data you're able to have difficult discussions, make plans, or hold organizations to account.

Q. *Do you have any advice for other communities trying to do similar projects?*

A. Having an external point of reference, access to data, community input, and continuous evaluation and learning has changed our journey. A number of people have learned more about deliberative practice, which has been invaluable for connecting community ideas to build solutions, and results have informed the learning journey. Community voices have provided a rich store of information to help change the status quo.

Having constant access to feedback and advice outside the city has been invaluable. An external point of reference has helped us to step back and retain a sense of independence, which has been important for facilitation. Remaining independent, but still connected to and understanding, the local issues has been an important learning point. The reason I was asked to chair Shine was that I am connected to and understand the local scene due to community participation in health matters. I'm a member and trustee of the New Zealand Social and Civic Policy Institute, which is directed by David Robinson. We meet every three months to touch base and deliberate with other like-minded organizations. That helps to refresh our thinking and provides an external point of reference.

And I think people going back and forth to Kettering, coming back with new energy and ideas, has actually been invaluable. That has helped us stop, get out of the quagmire, and reflect on what we're doing. It has also helped to build a critical mass of like-minded people. This is important.

Maureen Gillon, a trustee of the New Zealand Social and Civic Policy Institute, has had wide experience working and volunteering in a variety of community, academic, health, education, and local government organizations. Her particular interest is in engaging communities of interest in dialogue on matters important to all of them.

Maura Casey, a former New York Times *editorial writer, is an associate of the Kettering Foundation.*

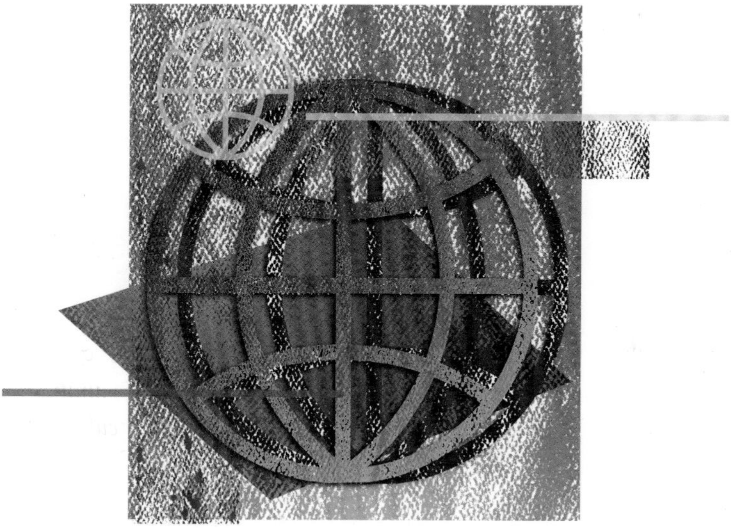